Making It in HOLLYWOOD

Behind the Success of **50** of Today's Favorite Actors, Screenwriters, Producers and Directors

Gail O'Donnell & Michele Travolta

Sourcebooks Inc.

Naperville, IL

Published by: **Sourcebooks, Inc.**
P.O. Box 372, Naperville, Illinois, 60566
(708) 961-3900
FAX: 708-961-2168

Editorial: John Santucci
Cover Design: Wayne Johnson
Interior Design: Wayne Johnson

This publication is designed to provide accurate and authoritative information in regard to the subject matter covered. It is sold with the understanding that the publisher is not engaged in rendering legal, accounting, or other professional service. If legal advice or other expert assistance is required, the services of a competent professional person should be sought.

From a Declaration of Principles Jointly Adopted by a Committee of the American Bar Association and a Committee of Publishers and Associations

Library of Congress Cataloging-in-Publication Data

Making it in hollywood : behind the success of more than 50 of today's
    favorite actors, writers, producers, and directors / [interviews by]
    Gail O'Donnell & Michele Travolta.
        p.   cm.
    ISBN 1-57071-015-5 : $24.95
    1. Motion picture industry—Vocational guidance.   2. Motion
pictures—Interviews.   I. O'Donnell, Gail, 1956–   II. Travolta
Michele, 1955–
PN1995.9.P75M29   1994
791.43'02'93--dc20
                                                        94-18450
                                                        CIP

Printed and bound in the United States of America
10 9 8 7 6 5 4 3 2 1

TABLE OF CONTENTS

FOREWORD xi

INTRODUCTION xiii

ACTORS 1

Jason Alexander 2

Seinfeld, Pretty Woman, North, The Paper

Scott Baio...8

Happy Days, Charles In Charge, Diagnosis: Murder

Robby Benson 12

Beauty and the Beast, Ice Castles, Jory, Harry and Son, The Chosen, The Godfather Part II

Barry Bostwick 16

The Rocky Horror Picture Show (Movie), Grease (Broadway), Scruples, George Washington, The Parent Trap II

Tim Curry...20

The Rocky Horror Picture Show (Play and Movie), The Hunt for Red October, Clue, Annie, The Three Musketeers, The Shadow

Davis Gaines 24

Phantom of the Opera

TABLE OF CONTENTS

Mariette Hartley..30

M.A.D.D.: The Candy Lightner Story, Silence of the Heart, Child of Rage

Ernie Hudson..34

*Ghostbusters, Ghostbusters II, The Crow, Airheads, Weeds, Sugar Hill,
No Escape, The Hand That Rocks the Cradle, The Cowboy Way*

Sally Kellerman 40

M.A.S.H., Boris and Natasha, Cousin Cousine, Back to School

Joey Lawrence 44

Blossom, Gimme a Break

Kathy Najimy..48

Sister Act, Sister Act 2, Hocus Pocus, The Fisher King

Michael Nouri..52

Flashdance, The Hidden, The Gangster Chronicles, Love and War

Sarah Jessica Parker..56

Honeymoon In Vegas, L.A. Story, Hocus Pocus, A Year in the Life

Joe Penny 62

Jake and the Fatman, Riptide, The Gangster Chronicles

Kelly Preston 66

Twins, Experts, Secret Admirer, Tiger's Tale

Alan Rachins 70

L.A. Law

Eric Roberts 76

*Star 80, The Pope of Greenwich Village, Runaway Train,
Final Analysis, The Ambulance, The Coca Cola Kid, The Specialist*

TABLE OF CONTENTS

Tom Skerritt..80

M.A.S.H., Alien, Top Gun, A River Runs Through It, Picket Fences

John Travolta..84

*Welcome Back Kotter, Saturday Night Fever, Grease, Pulp Fiction,
Urban Cowboy, Blow Out, Look Who's Talking (Parts I & II)*

Vanna White...88

Wheel of Fortune

Daphne Zuniga..92

*Melrose Place, The Sure Thing, Vision Quest, Gross Anatomy,
Spaceballs, Staying Together, The Fly II, The Last Rites*

SCREENWRITERS..97

Bob Gale..98

Back to the Future (Parts I, II & III), Trespass

Larry Hertzog..104

*Stephen Cannell Television, Hart to Hart, Walker: Texas Ranger,
Starbuck, Down Delaware Road, Tin Man*

David Koepp..108

*Death Becomes Her, Carlito's Way, Jurassic Park, The Paper,
The Shadow, Bad Influence, Apartment Zero*

Jim Kouf..114

*Stakeout (Parts I and II), Class, American Dreamer, Secret Admirer,
Disorganized Crime, Up the Creek, Miracles, The Hidden*

James Orr...120

*Three Men and A Baby, Sister Act 2, Mr. Destiny,
Father of the Bride (Producer)*

TABLE OF CONTENTS

Wesley Strick...124

Cape Fear, Final Analysis, True Believer, Arachnophobia, Wolf

James Toback 130

Bugsy, The Pick-Up Artist, Fingers

Daniel Waters...134

Batman Returns, Heathers, Demolition Man

DIRECTORS..141

Tony Bill 142

*Untamed Heart, Five Corners, Six Weeks, Crazy People, My Bodyguard,
A Home of Our Own, The Sting (Producer)*

Rob Bowman 148

*Star Trek: The Next Generation, Quantum Leap, Airborne,
Parker Lewis Can't Lose, Midnight Caller, Hat Squad*

James Bridges 152

*The Paper Chase, The China Syndrome, Bright Lights-Big City,
Urban Cowboy*

Marshall Herskovitz 158

Thirtysomething, Jack the Bear

Randal Kleiser 164

*Honey I Blew Up the Kid, Grease, The Gathering, White Fang,
The Blue Lagoon, Flight of the Navigator, Big Top Pee Wee*

Robert Lieberman 170

Fire in the Sky, Gabriel's Fire, Table for Five, All I Want for Christmas

TABLE OF CONTENTS

Nancy Malone...174

Melrose Place, Beverly Hills 90120, Dynasty, Falcon Crest,
The Long Hot Summer, Naked City

Jeff Margolis...180

Variety Specials, The Academy Awards, The American Music Awards

Russell Mulcahy...186

The Shadow, Highlander (Parts I & II), Ricochet

Frank Oz..190

Housesitter, The Muppets Take Manhattan, Dirty Rotten Scoundrels,
Little Shop of Horrors, What About Bob?

PRODUCERS...195

Lynn Bigelow..196

Another Stakeout (Stakeout II), Disorganized Crime, Kalifornia

Todd Black...200

Wrestling Ernest Hemingway, Fire in the Sky, Tough Guys,
Becoming Collette, Split Decisions, Short Time

Martin Bregman..206

Sea of Love, Serpico, The Shadow, Carlito's Way, Scarface,
Dog Day Afternoon, The Four Seasons

Larry Gershman..210

President of WIN (World International Network) Television

Dean Hargrove...214

Matlock, Perry Mason, Jake and the Fatman, Columbo

TABLE OF CONTENTS

Jonathan Krane 218

*Look Who's Talking, Look Who's Talking Now, The Chocolate War,
Micki and Maude, The Man Who Loved Women, Blind Date*

William Link...222

*Columbo, The Execution of Pvt. Slovik, That Certain Summer,
The Boys, The Bill Cosby Mysteries*

George Litto...226

Dressed to Kill, Blow Out, Obsession, Kansas

David Permut...230

*Consenting Adults, The Marrying Man, Captain Ron, Blind Date,
Three of Hearts, 29th Street, Dragnet*

Scott Sternberg...234

*The Newlywed Game, The Dating Game, Cable Television,
Variety Special: The Road to Hollywood*

Steve Tisch 238

*Forrest Gump, Risky Business, Bad Influence, The Burning Bed,
Corrina Corrina, Judgment, Afterburn, Outlaw Blues,*

Joe Wizan...244

*Jeremiah Johnson, And Justice for All, Tough Guys, Fire in the Sky,
Split Decisions, Wrestling Ernest Hemingway*

AFTERWORD 247

This book is dedicated to my lovely Nicole, whom I will always cherish.

Michele Travolta

This book is dedicated in memory of my mother, Anne Gradin.

Gail Gradin O'Donnell

In Memory of:

Rose Zouhire,

Grace Frazer,

James Bridges,

and

Dean Paul Martin

Our deepest thanks to Michael O'Donnell and Sam Travolta.

The authors wish to thank (in alphabetical order) the following people: Jacklynn Briskey, Rhonda Buha, Paula Peisner-Coxe, Roy Coxe, Janet Dart, Christopher Emerson, Allen Gradin, Joseph Green, Paul Haggar, Jodelle Hayes, Bob Isaian, Paul Isham, Michael Klawitter, Richard Marks, Tim Morgan, Charlie O'Donnell, Ellen Lerner O'Donnell, Heather Ross, Alexandra Sabella, Karin Storck, Richard Wellerstein, and all of the talented people who generously contributed their time and offered their insights on what it takes to make it in Hollywood.

FOREWORD

After all my years in the film business, I've come to one conclusion: You can't teach anyone how to make it in Hollywood. Having said that, Michele Travolta and Gail O'Donnell's book is the closest thing you can get to that end. They have compiled some of the best data, based on their hours of extensive interviews and research with some of the top names in the film and television industry.

Amidst anecdotes, advice and simple common sense, Michele and Gail's book truly delivers the goods with unedited, unabridged interviews straight from the horses' mouth. As you read each of these stories you will also begin to see that no two are the same. Everyone takes a different route on this hard but exciting road to Hollywood. And that's the beauty of it. In Hollywood there's still room to invent and reinvent yourself. *Making It In Hollywood* will give you the best tip of them all—read these stories, pick up what applies to you and then put it to work. I believe that Michele and Gail have truly created a book that will help to encourage and guide anyone interested in pursuing a career in Hollywood.

—Paul Haggar
Senior Vice President
Post Production
Paramount Pictures

INTRODUCTION

Filmmakers are a special kind of people. They are inspired individuals, reliant upon colleagues to bring their collective vision to the screen. *Making It In Hollywood* is a readable, accessible, all-purpose guide for aspiring entertainment visionaries, as well as for those people curious to learn who does what in bringing a film from concept to completion.

And who knows better than the people involved—actors, screenwriters, directors and producers—about what is actually involved? Through personal accounts of their careers, in their own words, these experienced veterans and popular newcomers reveal the subtle secrets to success: what it took to get "discovered"; getting representation; staying positive in spite of all the negatives; the rewards and frustrations of the business; the preparation it takes to succeed.

There are, unfortunately, no conclusive answers to the question, "What can I do to get a big break, to get discovered?" Earl Nightingale once said, "Luck is what happens when preparedness meets opportunity." In *Making It In Hollywood*, we've given you the keys to get you to that state of preparedness. Then, when the opportunity comes knocking, the door to realizing your dreams in the entertainment industry will swing wide and you'll be one of those "lucky" individuals.

If there are any common threads that bind these creative, successful people together, they are perseverance, persistence, and vision. If you have these qualities, along with a bit of guidance from this book, you just might be one of those "lucky" persons who makes it in Hollywood!

JASON ALEXANDER

Jason is probably best known for his portrayal of angst-ridden George Costanza on NBC's Seinfeld, *a role which has earned him two Emmy and two Golden Globe nominations, an American Television Award and two American Comedy Awards. His first film role was in* The Burning, *with newcomers Holly Hunter and Fisher Stevens. His subsequent filmwork included roles in* Brighton Beach Memoirs, The Mosquito Coast, White Palace, Coneheads, Pretty Woman, The Paper *and* North, *among others. He has appeared in many Broadway productions including* Jerome Robbins' Broadway, *for which he won a Tony award in 1989 for Best Actor in a Musical.*

How did your career begin?

I was always a fan of the theater and attended from a young age. I enjoyed listening to comedy albums, and I would memorize and repeat them to friends. Show albums were my favorite music and I knew entire scores by heart. When I was exposed to performing in school, I rallied to it. I loved it from the first time I set foot on a stage. As a result, I began studying voice and dance as a young teenager and participated in every kind of performance work I could find: lots of school plays, community theater, children's theater, etc.

It was while I was performing in the local children's theater group that a gentleman in the audience decided our little original shows might make good children's television. He produced two specials that starred our entire company. All of us had to join AFTRA to participate, so all of us became overnight professionals. The two specials aired, and though no one wanted to produce them for a series, they were seen with fairly good ratings in New York. Shortly after they aired, I received a call from a talent management office in New York and signed with them. They then spearheaded my career for the next eight years.

The uniqueness of my experience is that I did not, as most actors do, have to go hunting to find my representation. Miraculously, it came to me. I never faced that terrible time most actors face when they are left to pound sidewalks and doors, sending pictures, pleading for meetings just to get someone to believe in and help them. Had I had to face that, I don't know if I could have taken it.

JASON ALEXANDER

What was your training?

I started studying voice when I was twelve, and I started tap lessons at fourteen. I wanted to be the next Ben Vereen. Unreasonable, you think? I never had an acting lesson until I became a theater major at Boston University. I studied there for three years and then left because of numerous work offers. I continued training with a private coach named Larry Moss. I studied for six years straight with Larry and continue to be taught by him off and on to this day.

I know dozens of very successful, very talented actors who never had a lesson in their lives and who would probably not recommend them. But I believe that an actor who wishes to be prepared for a full spectrum of work and opportunity must study. To my amazement, at my first class I learned that there are actually tools and techniques to make performance richer, deeper, and more crafted. It is not just memorizing lines and blocking. It is not just doing a voice or walk. It is not just feeling it.

There are many teachers who are ignorant and destructive, but there are also many who can awaken and strengthen talents and resources you never knew you had. Find them. Use them. You will never lose what you already have, and you may discover a world you never dreamed of before.

When first starting your career, do you feel it is important to live in New York or L.A.?

There are advantages to living in these cities. They are the financial centers of the commercial aspect of the business. Most commercial projects originate there, so these cities support many of the sub-sidiary interests of the actor: agents, managers, casting directors, teachers, etc. Also, if your dreams are to appear on Broadway or to be a TV and/or movie actor, these cities may be your only bet. However, acting goes on all over the country and all over the world.

What kind of actor do you want to be? Must you be a movie star? Do you want to play the classics? Do you want to bring theater to children? Do you want to be part of avant-garde or political pieces? These are questions you must answer for yourself before you decide where to pursue your career. There is work everywhere. International stardom is only in New York and L.A., and I'm not sure everyone wants or needs international stardom.

What advice would you give to someone working full time and pursuing an acting career?

First, be honest. If there is anything else you can do and be relatively happy—note I did not say *ecstatically* happy—do it! This profession is only for those who have no choice; they must do this for there is nothing else they can do. If you have options, I promise your life will be happier if you pursue them. Act by all means, but just not professionally. You may find it just as rewarding.

However, if this is what you live and die for, keep going. Keep studying. Invite fellow actors over and do play readings. Try some improvisation. Do small charity shows at hospitals or schools. Write. Sing. Do stand-up. Keep performing! You are an actor, not a waiter. Act, act, act!

Don't wait around to be discovered, or for a big break. Own your career. Option properties. Develop writing. Make videos. Do cabaret. Don't wait for someone to give you permission to do what you do—you'll be a bitter eighty-year-old. Do it now. Yes, go through all the bullshit with pictures and submissions and open calls and apprenticeships, but do this, too: empower yourself. Perform and the powers that be will come to you. Make them see who you are through your work. It can be done.

Most actors think auditions are hell. I love them. To me they are a one-night-only performance of a role I think I can do better than anyone else. They are opportunities to meet other people in the business that I admire. I have reached a place in my career where I am not always asked to audition, but rather, I'm given the role. I hate it! I'd rather everyone else see what my take on the role is so that there are no "artistic differences" later.

To explain how I prepare for auditions would be to go heavily into my technique and I have neither the time nor the clarity of mind to do that here. Maybe that will be my book, someday. But emotionally, you must show up. You—the real you—must come through the door. Dress the part? Sure, why not. Really go for it when you read? Absolutely. But come in as a human being and meet the other human beings in the room. Assume that everyone who auditions is talented. Sometimes people get jobs because everyone wants to be around them. Exude confidence and craft. Don't be afraid. They want you to be great. They may be spending millions of dollars to mount a project. They're more nervous than you. They want the perfect person to walk through the door. Why not have it be you? Go get it.

Can you explain the difference between film and stage acting?

Yes...there is none. The work an actor does is always the same whether in preparation for a stage, a musical, a commercial, a Shakespeare role, children's theater, sitcom or dramatic film. Your technique is your technique and the resulting performance is holy and should not be altered for different mediums.

JASON ALEXANDER

Some people will tell you, "You must play small on film." Well, if Steve Martin had done that he'd have no career. Others say, "You can't do beat-by-beat work on a sitcom." The fact is, if you ever want to work anywhere except on a sitcom, you'd better do beat-by-beat work while you're on it, or no one will believe you're an actor.

The only thing that changes in a performance is the space the performance must fill. A 5,000-seat theater will require a different performance energy than a passionate love scene in a film. But that's all. The other differences between film and television are technical and easily learned within hours of beginning work on them. Tell the director or assistant director it's your first time—they'll treat you like a virgin. Otherwise, don't concern yourself with technical differences. Leave it to the tech guys. Just do your work. You're part of the process. The director will integrate you. Don't worry about it.

How do you face rejection?

It's never easy. The fact is you may be rejected for height, ethnicity, vocal range, type, age, or the fact that they really want a star, or the producer has a girlfriend. There is also the possibility that you really gave a shitty audition.

Know who you are. How do you fit into the spectrum of talent that's out there? Are you a leading actor or a character type? Are you physically right for the role? Are you seeing yourself clearly? Don't get too excited about the roles that are a long shot. But also know your ability. Do you play comedy effectively? Can you handle the language of the classics? Can you express your emotions with facility? Did you do all the preparation you could for the audition or meeting? Are your skills honed? Are you a craftsman or a hack? Be honest. Be the best actor you can be. Be realistic.

Understand the enormity of the competition. Make each opportunity a full one and don't kill yourself over the blown ones. And again, have your own thing. Not getting one job is easily gotten over when you're going to another, particularly if it's one you created.

How do you get an agent?

There are no tricks. Persistence. Pictures. Calls. Auditions. As I've stressed, having something they can see you in works wonders.

What do you look for when choosing a project?

I am only just reaching the point where I can afford to be choosy in what I do. Usually you look for a paycheck, a connection, or a piece of film for your reel as reason enough to do a job. That's where

99.9% of all actors are in their careers. Only recently have I had enough financial security that I can begin to etch my career as well as my craft. So I look for something that I think will either entertain, educate or stimulate a large audience.

I have always been an actor of the people. I love audiences and I feel an obligation to them. I'd like them to think if they're paying to see me it will be worth it. I also look for a challenge: What scares me about the role? And the joy: What excites or delights me about the role?

Who else is involved? My career is moving more into direction because I am so tired of directors who have no skill or craft, who can't communicate, have no vision, or worse—no common sense. I look very closely at the directors and I ask myself, "Is this worth being away from my family?" More and more, if the answer is "no," I don't do it.

What are the most frustrating and most gratifying parts of being an actor?

Most frustrating is the lack of tenure. You work and work, you make a reputation, you achieve a level of respect and recognition and compensation and tomorrow it can be gone. "Oh, he does TV—we can't use him for film." "Oh, he sings, so he's not a serious actor." "Oh, he was in two bad films in a row—he's box office poison." The bullshit is limitless. I want tenure. You succeed for twenty years, you become a partner, fully vested in the pension plan, and all the junior partners come to you for advice and counsel.

The most gratifying has always been and remains the audience. I have always been blessed with being able to do the thing I love most and, at the same time, bring so much joy to people. They have always been so kind to me and expressed their pleasure so profoundly. Thanks to film and TV, that audience has increased a thousandfold, but the kindness and appreciation remain the same.

How do you sustain a career?

Keep working on your craft, keep learning, and stay real and humble. You are never as great as they are telling you. Don't buy into the fantasy aspect of the business—it's giddy but false. Just do your work as best you know how.

SCOTT BAIO

Scott received his first real break when director Garry Marshall saw him in the movie Bugsy
Malone *and cast him as "Chachi Arcola" in the popular television series* Happy Days, *which
turned him into a teen sensation. He reprised that role in his next series,* Joanie Loves Chachi.
His television success continued with the long-running series Charles in Charge *and* Diagnosis:
Murder, *with Dick Van Dyke.*

Would you briefly explain how you got started in your career?

I was an avid television watcher, and I decided television was something I wanted to pursue. I
had a cousin who was very popular in New York, so I went and met his agent, who took an
interest in me and got me started in commercial work.

So you started in commercials?

Yes. I did a commercial for a magazine called *Age of Discovery*, but I quit [doing commercials]
because I did not like going into Manhattan. My agent then called me and sent me to read for a
film called *Bugsy Malone*. I got the part when I was thirteen. That was my first real break.

When did you start Happy Days?

Two Years later. Garry Marshall saw me in *Bugsy Malone* and brought me out to L.A. I did a show
before *Happy Days* called *Blanksy Beauties,* with Nancy Walker, and then went into *Happy Days.*

Is there anything in particular that you look for when choosing a project?

Something well-written. It sounds corny, but if it's not well-written, it's a waste of time. There's a
saying, "If it's not on the page, it's not on the stage." So I would have to say good writing, a good
story, and a good character.

SCOTT BAIO

What is your opinion of acting classes?

For myself, I don't necessarily believe in classes, but whatever works for somebody is helpful. If you are going to take a class, I would recommend an improvisation class taught by Helaine Lembeck. I took an improvisation class her father, Harvey Lembeck, used to teach. It keeps you tuned, it keeps your mind working, and it makes you think when you're onstage.

Since you've done both television and film work, what is the difference?

The difference is the hours. It's more time-consuming doing a movie than doing a half-hour show. It's more grueling and taxing. But then again there's the positive, which is you get that special performance, you get the close-ups, you get to take your time—you get all those things that you dream about doing, whereas in a half-hour show, it's like running: you have fun doing it and you just fly by the seat of your pants. It really depends on what you like to do.

How do you prepare for auditions?

I just read the script. You've got to figure out who the character is that you're playing. I try to memorize the dialogue and say it out loud several times. Going over it with somebody has always been helpful for me. So when you feel comfortable and it sounds like you're saying it right, then you're ready.

How do you sustain your career?

I think it is easier in television rather than films. If you're a movie star and you do two bad movies, it's rough. If you do a series and you do two bad episodes, nobody cares. It's much harder to be a movie star for a long time than it is a television star. I don't want to downplay the other, I think you just have to do what you think is good and you feel is right. It's hard to be smart. You have to out-think everybody and be ahead of everybody, and that can be very tiring

What advice would you give someone who has to work full time in another profession while at the same time pursuing his or her career goal?

If you can get a job in the business that pays your bills, go ahead because you'll learn more that way than being a waiter.

What suggestions can you give with regard to obtaining representation?

Get involved in a workshop that puts on small performances. Equity waiver plays are always good because so often, agents are looking for new talent.

In the face of rejection, how do you maintain a sense of security?

I try not to get excited about anything. So if I read for something, I try to forget about it. If you get the part, it's fine; if you don't, then you've forgotten about it. You don't get dejected. For me, I don't allow myself to get excited about anything until I actually do it.

What is the most frustrating and then the most gratifying part of being an actor?

The most frustrating is directors who don't know what they're doing, and bad writing. Gratifying is when something works, when you finish a show and you look at it and it's good. Attention from your fans is gratifying in the beginning, and that's always gratifying. But that has its own place. There were times I couldn't walk down the street. It's incredibly intoxicating. Also gratifying is working with somebody that's good and that you have good chemistry with—that's great.

What further advice would you give a person getting started in acting?

First find out if you can act or not. If you can, then go to class if you feel it's necessary. Take an improv or a workshop class, something that you can show off what you do. You have to work very hard. You can't do it for the fame. You really can't. You've got to do it because you love it.

At this stage of your career, what are your greatest challenges?

I guess the challenge is just to keep working. It's not that easy. I would like to direct a series for a couple of years...that would be great fun.

ROBBY BENSON

Robby Benson's acting career started at age five, when he began performing in summer stock productions with his mother. His Broadway debut came at age twelve in the play Zelda. *Robby got his break in films at age fourteen in the 1971 production of* Jeremy. *Since then, he has starred in such films as* One on One, Ice Castles, The Godfather Part II, Harry and Son, *and many others, including the Disney animated feature* Beauty and the Beast, *where he was the voice of the Beast. In addition to acting, Robby writes and directs, and has taught courses in filmmaking and screen acting at the University of South Carolina. He recently taught graduate level film and television acting at UCLA [University of California, Los Angeles], and a new film program started by Robby at the University of Utah features him as a visiting professor.*

Would you briefly explain how you got started in your career?

My father was in the cotton business and while working in the plant, he would write satire and political review. It played in Dallas, Texas. He produced and directed the shows. My mother would perform in the shows, and they became incredibly successful. I literally grew up in rehearsal halls and nightclubs. My father also wrote for comics.

When I was five years old, I did my first commercial and moved on to summer stock, performing in shows that my mom starred in. When I was about seven, I would sell popcorn, help with the lights, show people to their seats, and paint scenery. From that point on, we moved to New York because my father's writing career took off, and I just never stopped working. I costarred in my first Broadway show, called *Zelda*, when I was twelve years old. Then I did the *Rothchild's*. I got my first film lead in *Jory* when I was fourteen. Then I worked on a little film called *Jeremy*, which I helped write, but did not get screen credit. I continued to write and sold my first screenplay when I was eighteen to Warner Brothers. That was *One On One*, and that I cowrote with my father.

ROBBY BENSON

Did you have any formal acting training?

No, just "on-the-job training." I would say theater was the most important training ground for me, and still is. Discipline. Nothing takes the place of discipline...and respect for the work and the people around you.

What do you look for when choosing a project?

There are a lot of things I look for when choosing a project. But careers go in cycles, and there have been times when I've done things that I wouldn't normally do because this is not only my craft, but it's the way I make a living for my family. The reality is when you are doing extremely well and you can look for the kinds of projects you believe in and that you want to be a part of. You look for projects that will last forever and make people want to go to the movies or the theater. Those are the kinds of projects I'd like to be involved with, but it doesn't always work out that way.

How do you prepare for an audition?

You have to be very focused. I believe that you never want to lose your hunger. It doesn't matter how successful you are, you can't lose your drive. I have also been on the other side of the audition process. The most important element is to never lose your desire.

How did **Beauty and the Beast** *come about for you?*

That was just luck! I was teaching film at the University of South Carolina for two years. I had actually thought I was going to leave the film business for good, but when I came back to Los Angeles, there was a call asking me if I would be interested in doing the project. I had done voice work since I was a little boy. I got really excited about it because of my daughter. I thought, "My God! I can be in a Disney movie, and to my daughter, that would be like winning the 'daddy lottery!'" So I auditioned five times and got lucky enough to get it.

Is it important for someone just starting out to live in New York or Los Angeles?

It is very important. My favorite time in my career was summer stock, but being in New York made all the difference in the world. New York was "cutthroat" and that experience taught me what was necessary to win or get a job.

What advice would you give someone who has to work full-time while pursuing acting?

If you are a family person and you have responsibilities, you must have that steady job. If not, I would say go for broke and devote every second of your life to your act.

How does one sustain a career in this industry?

For one thing, you need to be thick-skinned. At the same time, your goals and dreams have to stay intact. Make sure your dreams are not destroyed. Perseverance is very important. You also have to be able to battle back, heal quickly. Don't dwell on rejection, learn from it.

What additional advice would you give someone just starting out?

People get into this business because they want to make a lot of money, or they want to be famous. Those people will have their dreams destroyed quickly...they are in the business for the wrong reasons. There may be some perks in there, but even so, I don't think they will be happy because the only thing that keeps you going is your art. You must love the art more than anything else.

What is the most frustrating and then the most gratifying part of being an actor?

The most frustrating is the business itself. I often say to myself, "I can't wait to leave the business," but I feel so at home when I'm working. It's all I know. I have been doing this for so long. The most rewarding thing is the constant challenge. You never really get it right. Maybe there are some—Meryl Streep or Robert De Niro or Dustin Hoffman—who get it right, but other people need to work harder. It's more and more difficult to make something very interesting. The challenge is to make something play so beautifully that audiences will never question your credibility. They'll just enjoy themselves.

At this stage of your career, what are your greatest challenges?

Staying alive! Some things have gone full circle. I went through hell about nine years ago when I had open-heart surgery. I was at the height of my career, and it was as if the whole world came tumbling down on me. Now my biggest goal is to make sure my family is okay. That is my only goal.

BARRY BOSTWICK

Barry Bostwick made his screen debut in the classic cult film The Rocky Horror Picture Show. *His other film credits include* Megaforce, Weekend at Bernie's 2, *and* Movie, Movie. *On television, he has appeared in* Scruples, George Washington, A Woman of Substance, War & Remembrance, Till We Meet Again, Deceptions, Murder By Natural Cause, Body of Evidence, *and more. Onstage, Barry is credited with originating the role of "Danny Zuko" in the Broadway Smash* Grease.

How did you begin your career?

I started acting in high school in plays and community theater. I attended college in San Diego at California Western and got my Bachelor's Degree in Fine Arts. While in college, I worked every summer doing summer stock. I got my equity card working on a production of *Take Her, She's Mine* with Walter Pidgeon. By my third year I was cast with APA Phoenix Repertory Company. I was then asked to join the company, which I did. Later I decided then to go back to school at NYU School of the Arts. In New York, I studied with Olympia Dukakis. She was one of my favorite teachers. I started doing off Broadway until my first big hit, which was *Grease* in 1972 in which I created the part of "Danny Zuko." The first film I did that was released nationally was *The Rocky Horror Picture Show,* in which I played the role of Brad.

What suggestions can you give with regard to obtaining representation?

Use any contact that you have to it's fullest. Try and create ways for yourself to be tireless. This business requires a total obsession in the beginning, then after you make a name for yourself or you have gotten at least a mechanics set up around you that could keep you afloat for awhile, then you could relax and do what I think is the next important thing in your life and that is to develop hobbies.

BARRY BOSTWICK

What is the most frustrating and then the most gratifying aspect of being an actor?

The most frustrating is when you have to think as to what level you are in with regards to your career. Every level has it's own set of frustrations. In the beginning finding an agent was frustrating. It's also frustrating when you don't use all the tools that you have spent the last five or six years toning. You sort of go into this fog for awhile.

The most gratifying is coming up with ways to be seen. It's a classic story in this industry with actors who pass the envelope, in terms of doing oddball, risky, or interesting things to be seen by producers, directors, or agents. I encourage that [for] the first six to eight years of your career—you cannot wait for it to happen to you. And if you do, you are not going to make it because there is too much competition, particularly right now. There are many schools pumping out new actors who have enthusiasm and the right vows needed to make it in this business.

When faced with rejection, how did you maintain a sense of security?

I didn't. It's very difficult. That is why I think you need a strong team around you. You need at least one person—a manager, agent, lawyer, business manager—someone who knows the business, the ups and downs, and knows how this business is. I think you have to become very spiritual. It reaches a point where spirituality is your rock—and that doesn't mean religion. It just means that you need some sense of spirituality in your life. Once you accept that everyone has their own path in their career—that their win is not your loss—but that takes a lot of work. Whatever spiritual path you choose to follow...mine was meditation. I found myself. It was the way to stay well, calm, and to keep things in perspective. I have meditated since 1975.

Is there anything you look for when choosing a project?

I look for one that is offered to me! I don't think there are many of us that have the opportunity to choose. You choose to do it or not. Every project I do, there is some reason for me to do it. It could be for money or to work with certain people now and in the future...networking. Or I often do projects because I like the script. Perhaps it was written by someone interesting, and the character does something that I've never done before—I have the opportunity to explore myself. Or perhaps the character capitalizes on attributes that I am developing and this is who I am. It will seem very real.

How did you prepare for auditions?

In the beginning I would try and find something that was so off-the-wall just to be noticed. Ringling Brothers Circus was putting together this group to be like a pop group. I was a sunflower, so I cut a big piece of cardboard to look like a sunflower and put it over my head and my face came popping through. I walked into the room singing *"Here Comes The Sun King."* I got the part! That's the kind of thing that you have to do when you are starting out. You have to think of the wackiest, silliest, yet interesting things you can do.

What further advice would you give an aspiring actor?

Stay humble. Don't burn your bridges, and on the other hand, don't be so concerned about everybody liking you. I think that show business is just a metaphor for the world, and if you are in this business for approval, you are not going to be a star. You have to develop a strong center, a strong sense of self-confidence and the ability to go against other people's wishes and cutdowns. Your agent or manager or the director—whomever—may want you to do something one way and your instinct says, "I don't want to do it this way." You have to fight for the way you want to do it. That is the only way you will end up a unique individual.

At this stage of your career, what are your greatest challenges?

Maintaining the level I'm at and trying to jump into another level. I think everyone has this problem. The roof is always higher. I've been a very slow builder in my career. I do it step-by-step. I didn't plan it this way, it's just the way it turned out. I once said to myself early on, "What I really want to be in this business is a 'citizen actor.'" I want to be someone who will work for the rest of their lives and do interesting projects and not necessarily always play the lead.

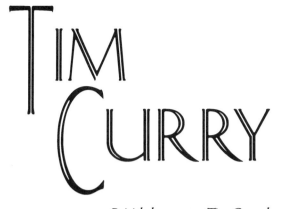

TIM CURRY

British-born actor Tim Curry has created a rich array of memorable characters, both for the screen and the stage. He made his professional debut in the West End production of Hair, *then went on to appear in a Scottish opera company tour of* A Midsummer Night's Dream *and several other productions before landing his famous role in the highly acclaimed stage production of* The Rocky Horror Picture Show *as Dr. Frank N. Furter. Tim starred in the musical in both New York and Los Angeles before returning to England to make his film debut in the motion picture adaptation. He has appeared in other Broadway productions, including Tom Stoppard's* Travesties, Me and My Girl, *and as Mozart in* Amadeus, *for which he received a Tony Award nomination for Best Actor. His film credits include* The Hunt for Red October, Home Alone 2, Clue, The Three Muskateers, Legend, Annie, *and most recently* The Shadow, *with Alec Baldwin.*

How did you begin your career?

I earned a B.A. degree in English and Drama at Birmingham University in England and talked my way into the London production of *Hair* in 1968.

What advice would you give to someone pursuing an acting career?

You'd better want it badly, because they rarely want you.

What do you look for when choosing a project?

I'm happiest at the left of center. I look for writing that has a language of its own. I rarely find it.

Did you have formal training?

Not really...a few notional acting classes at the university. I learned on my feet and by observing other people.

TIM CURRY

Would you recommend acting schools, and if so, which ones?

It's probably a good idea, if only because they tend to have professional connections. I'm not sufficiently aware of them to make a recommendation.

What advice would you give an aspiring actor regarding how to handle rejection while maintaining a sense of security?

Can you give me some?

Explain the audition process and how you prepare for auditions.

The process is arbitrary at best and humiliating at worst. Basically you have to—in the words of Tyrone Guthrie—"astonish them with your gifts." It is useful only in that it helps you to become aware of the qualities that set you apart, that are unique to you. Try to surprise, but not at the cost of the material.

How does one obtain representation?

Try begging, then...a little arrogance.

Is it imperative that an aspiring actor live in L.A. or New York?

Pretty much, not only because almost everything is cast from one place or the other, but also you will need the support (or competition) from other actors, the community. However, ignore provincial theatre at your peril.

Are film schools beneficial to an aspiring actor?

I don't know. It's probably useful to understand the technical problems involved. I pester film crews all the time in order to figure out what they're doing. But time spent at film school is time spent not acting, and the best way to learn is by doing.

What is the most frustrating and then the most gratifying part of being an actor?

Actors are victims of fashion and other people's perception of them. It's gratifying to create your own and defy those perceptions and to embody the extraordinarily complex poetry of human behavior. Plus, you can do it 'til you die.

What advice would you give someone who has to work a full-time job while pursuing acting?

Take a part-time job and starve a little.

How much rehearsal is necessary when preparing for a shoot?

It depends on the role. I don't like to rehearse much for film, because the camera captures the spontaneity of response, the dawning of an idea, what is going on behind your eyes—it relishes contradiction. I try to be brave enough to fly blind.

How does one sustain a career in the industry?

Surprise. Reliability. Trusting your instincts. The brave choice.

At this stage of your career, what are your greatest challenges or aspirations?

What they always were: to reveal to an audience something human of which they were previously unaware...to tell the truth...to be able still to pay for my garden.

Any further advice?

Try gardening. Try to astonish.

DAVIS GAINES

Davis made his Broadway debut in the chorus of Camelot, *with Sir Richard Burton, and later as "Raoul" in the Broadway production of* The Phantom of the Opera. *He has performed in the national tours of* The Best Little Whorehouse in Texas, *with Alexis Smith, and* Hello, Dolly! *with Carol Channing. Davis has been featured in a number of network television dramas, including CBS's* Bodies of Evidence *and* Murder She Wrote. *He recently completed a role in the feature film* Warlock II: The Armageddon *and is fresh off of his record-breaking run of 942 performances as the Phantom in the Los Angeles production of* The Phantom of the Opera. *Davis is an ardent supporter of a variety of AIDS charities and is the national spokesperson for the Asthma and Allergy Foundation of America.*

How did you get started in your career?

I wanted to be an actor from my earliest recollection. There wasn't much in Orlando, Florida for me to do in that direction at the time. I scoured the area to find things to do, and I found a children's theater group when I was really young and stayed with them for a few years. From that, I did local plays and continued taking drama in Junior High and High School. I took tap classes, but my voice was a natural thing. About two years ago, I won a grant to study voice, which forced me to find a teacher, so now I have a technique. Before that, I was "natural." My first big show was on Broadway in *Camelot* with Richard Burton.

When did Phantom come about for you?

I had been in the Broadway production of *Phantom* two years ago as "Raoul," the love-interest character. When I was there, they saw my work, then called me when this opening came up in Los Angeles. I had to audition and I got the part of the Phantom. They took a chance on me and I worked out! I've been in the show the longest of any of the Phantoms.

DAVIS GAINES

How do you maintain a sense of security in the face of rejection?

I don't know if I do, but that's what it's all about. You have to accept the rejection. Otherwise, you can't make it—you can't do this business. You get many more rejections than you get acceptances. You have to be able to say, "I did my best and if they didn't go for it, then fine—move on to the next thing."

How should an actor get representation?

Be involved in a project where agents can come see your work, whether it be a showcase, equity waiver or student film. To be seen is essential!

If an actor has to work a "day job" while pursuing his craft, what jobs would be the most beneficial?

I've never had to do that. I've been lucky enough to be able to work in this business the whole time. I would suggest, however, to have your days free. Get an evening job, or hope to have a very understanding boss who let's you go out on auditions when needed. You need something flexible. Things happen so fast in Los Angeles, so your schedule would have to be very flexible.

How much rehearsal is needed for a show like **Phantom**?

Rehearsal is a lot longer in theater than in television or film. For a Broadway show, rehearsals range from four to eight weeks. Most shows that you do in regional theaters have a four-week rehearsal. Once a show starts, you rarely have a rehearsal. In *Phantom*, there is an understudy rehearsal every two weeks. However, rarely do we have a company rehearsal unless something is going wrong or something needs to be changed.

What film or television work have you done?

I have just done my first feature called *Warlock II*. As far as television work goes, I started in New York doing soap operas, and in Los Angeles, a CBS series called *Bodies of Evidence*. I have also recently completed an episode of *Murder, She Wrote*.

What do you look for when choosing a project?

I always try to do something that I haven't done before...something new and exciting. I look for a project that will help me grow personally as well as professionally as an actor. I try to learn something from each project and take it to the next one. I try not to go backwards and repeat things over and over again.

What is the most frustrating and then the most gratifying part of being an actor?

The most frustrating is getting a job, but not necessarily for your talent. You may get a job because of the color of your hair, the way you look, how tall you are, or being in the right place at the right time, or who you know. You can't just go on talent alone—you can't imagine all the things that go into the process of choosing an actor. The most rewarding for me is right now, doing *Phantom*: being onstage every night in that incredible role and being able to move people and touch their emotions and see them respond to that. It is really exciting.

How do you prepare for auditions?

For musical auditions, I usually sing things that I'm really comfortable with and I don't have to think about, so that I can let go and "do my thing." In film and television, it's a whole different ball of wax! I have found that I need to be really prepared. I need to be overly prepared with the script, and so once again, I can let go and play the moment instead of worrying about the words I am talking about, or trying to read the paper. The most important thing I try to do is to be familiar with the material instead of totally memorizing it.

Why did you become an actor?

I became an actor for a lot of reasons. When I was a child, I was very shy and introverted and would play pretend during the day, like all little kids do. I found that I could perform or become another character and not have to deal with the insecurities I had as a child. After awhile when I was doing that, I would get feedback from an audience. As a young person, that filled up the void of the insecurities of wanting to be accepted. Actually then I became good at it, then it just snowballed. I love the actual work of it, and now that I am doing it, I find that there is more to it than just the applause or becoming another character. I don't feel the need to hide behind anything anymore. It's work. You get to create the characters and figure out the best way to portray them. You get to affect people in different ways. It's not just for fun anymore, like it was as a child. It's a job now.

Is there some part of you in the character of the Phantom?

You always bring something of yourself to a character. I try to find a sense of humor in the characters I portray. The Phantom is very serious for the most part, but I still find places I can make him have a sense of humor. I feel when you show humor in a character, it makes it more "real."

DAVIS GAINES

How do you sustain a career as an actor?

I have been very lucky in my life as an actor. I haven't really had to do other jobs on the side to make money or support myself. I've worked in the theater all my life. That's encouraging and also rare. So far, I haven't had trouble sustaining myself as as actor. Just remember, a celebrity is no different than anyone else. It's just that people recognize you and you need to keep both sides in perspective. Don't forget where you came from.

Does an aspiring actor or actress have to live in New York or Los Angeles when first starting his or her career?

If you want to be in theater, New York is the place to be. Film and TV work is in Los Angeles. There are also wonderful classes in L.A. that teach you the right technique for film and television work.

At this stage of your career, what are your greatest challenges?

To keep working and try to originate a role of my own on Broadway. I am excited about the prospect of doing other things and branching out and seeing what happens. There are no doors that I have closed.

MARIETTE HARTLEY

At age fourteen, Mariette became the protegé of Eva La Gallienne and John Houseman. She starred in A Winter's Tale *and* A Midsummer Night's Dream *at the Stratford Shakespeare Festival and* The Merchant of Venice *at the Goodman Theatre in Chicago. Her first film role was in Sam Peckinpah's* Ride the High Country, *which netted her a seven-year contract from MGM and parts in* Marnie, Skyjacked *and* Encino Man. *She has appeared many times on television in shows such as* Peyton Place, Goodnight Beantown, *and* The Incredible Hulk, *which earned her an Emmy Award. Television movies such as* The Last Hurrah, M.A.D.D.: The Candy Lightner Story, *and her highly popular Polaroid commercials with James Garner have made her face familiar to millions. She became a best-selling author with the publication of her autobiography* Breaking the Silence. *Currently, she can be seen in the critically acclaimed Los Angeles production of* The Sisters Rosenzweig.

How did your career begin?

I started when I was ten years old in Westport, Connecticut. There was a wonderful children's production of *Jack and the Beanstalk* that I begged my mother to take me to see. We saw it, and I watched those kids who were my age looking like they were having the time of their lives. At that moment, I knew that that is what I wanted to do.

I then became a member of that group which was called The Silver Nutmeg Theater. My first production was *Alice in Wonderland,* and I can remember I had to literally be pushed on stage. I was so scared. But once I got out, you could not get me to go back in. From that time on, I really never stopped. I toured around Connecticut with *Little Women.* Those children's theaters were wonderful and I recommend them to anybody. That is really where the joy began for me and where the discipline began, which is very important.

From that time, I studied with a woman named Eva La Gallienne, who was a brilliant teacher, actor, and producer. She was one of the first people to start repertory companies in the United States and do public pricing—people like Joseph Papp and John Houseman used to see her productions in New York. She had a lot to do with people's early beginnings. I talk about her in my book, *Breaking the Silence.* Then I went to Carnegie Tech. After that, I met John Houseman, who gave me a scholarship to study at the Shakespeare Festival. I began performing and went on

MARIETTE HARTLEY

tour. I came out to Hollywood in 1961, and by a fluke, met Sam Peckinpah and did his first major film before *The Wild Bunch*, called *Ride the High Country*. I had a very hard time from then on, until the Polaroid commercials. So those are basically the "throes of my career."

What suggestions can you give someone who has to work full-time while pursuing an acting career?

Don't give up your day job. I don't know if you can have a nine-to-five job and work in this business. Ultimately, it becomes one or the other, and you have to risk one or the other. There are no real safety nets. If actors need to supplement their income, they become waiters, cab drivers...not everyone has a subsidy, so you really have to weigh it out.

How do you prepare for auditions?

You read the script and prepare. I don't memorize, mostly because you don't get the script in time to memorize, or it's such a long scene, that there is no way to memorize. A lot of times, I will go to an acting coach.

From one actor to another, I feel we come into readings with a certain amount of anger and fear combined! When you go to audition, I think you need a certain amount of humility. You cannot go in with a chip on your shoulder. The other thing I do is in my mind: I put a light in the room before I go in. What this does is grace the space, and this is very helpful for me.

In the face of rejection, how do you maintain a sense of security?

I think the older I am, the rejection gets worse. This has been a very rough year for me, rejectionwise. My family is a great help, which makes me grateful for having them. I also believe if you have something outside acting, whether you are single or not, that will help a great deal. We need to find fulfilling things, and I don't necessarily mean a day job. Writing is a great outlet. If you think you have talent, get yourself a computer or just write in longhand. So, finding something else to do is vital.

I also think actors are trained for rejection. I have a friend who tells me to rely on the body of work. And I keep saying to people, "If you are rejected, don't buy the myth that you deserve to be rejected." It's very difficult to get rejected day after day and, as an actor, you are. So you must know this going in. I feel when we are rejected, we must go back to our hearts.

What do you look for when choosing a project?

I have been very lucky to do parts that have social meaning. Those kind of parts have come to me ever since I did *M.A.D.D.: The Candy Lightner Story*. Then I did *Silence of the Heart* and *Child of*

Rage. I seem to do pretty much issue-oriented pieces. I also feel a sense of responsibility comes with my visibility, which is probably an overdeveloped conscience. I am also a parent, and I want my children to be proud of me.

The flip side is that I love comedy; the bottom line is that I look for a good script with a lot of different levels. Being onstage is the best way to be on different kinds of levels. I also look for something risky and something I haven't done before.

What are the most frustrating and gratifying parts of being an actor?

What comes to my mind is being myself. I do a whole monologue in my one-woman show on Meryl Streep called *Here a Streep, There a Streep, Everywhere a Streep.* This starts back in 1981 when she was on the cover of everything. The irony of that is true: we keep growing into ourselves. Everyday I learn something about myself—my strengths and weaknesses. My strength can be myself and my weakness can be myself. So the most frustrating thing is having people not know who I am, and that is one of the reasons that I started doing my one-woman show. People have a tendency to typecast. The frustrating part is trying to convince people that I can do this—something that is different.

Another thing that is frustrating—not speaking about myself per se—is that there are so many talented people out there that can't even get a chance to be seen. They can't get past "those offices" to show the talent they have. That is very frustrating.

The most gratifying is doing good work that I feel good about. I love the theater, so being onstage has been extremely rewarding for me. I also have written a book, and I go and speak all over the country. Even though I do all kinds of things other than this business, it is still in the communication field, and those things are very gratifying.

Any further advice?

Be flexible, be willing as actors, and keep praying. Don't loose faith in ourselves or respect for ourselves.

At this stage of your career, what are your greatest challenges?

Trying not to buy the myth that "the older you are, the harder it is to work." Also trying to keep my sights on the good parts. Acceptance is the key, in a sense, and a belief in my body of work and enough money to ride through the rough times—and to be able to keep my foot in the door and never stop. I always want to be prepared for the next role. The wonderful thing about my one-woman show is that I always have to be prepared. These are some of my greatest challenges right now.

ERNIE HUDSON

Ernie Hudson's extensive credits are a testimony to his fine work, including his rich portrayal of "Solomon," the mentally impaired workman/hero in The Hand That Rocks the Cradle. *Other credits include the world-popular* Ghostbusters *and* Ghostbusters II. *One of his favorite roles was as "Bagdad Everhardt" in the film* Weeds *(with Nick Nolte), where he delivered an emotionally charged performance. He has recently been seen in such films as* Sugar Hill, No Escape, The Crow, The Cowboy Way, *and* Airheads. *Ernie has also just completed a role in* Speechless, *with Geena Davis and Michael Keaton.*

How did your career begin?

I started acting in college at Wayne State University in Detroit. I got married at age eighteen and we had a son. I desperately wanted to get a good job. After working several jobs, and many that could be classified as "good jobs," I realized I could not do the nine-to-five routine. It then dawned on me that I wasn't going to be successful doing anything other than acting. I then started to do a lot of theater in college, and local regional theater—and that's how I got started.

What advice would you give someone just starting out?

That's always a hard question to answer and one I get asked a lot. Every case is unique and different. Things that other people were encouraged by were very discouraging to me. I have always recommended that you have to make a commitment to this profession. I am very big on commitments. Once you make a total commitment to acting, it will, in turn, totally support you. My other advice would be isolate and work on your weaknesses. If you have a great smile and smile a lot but don't work on your squeaky voice…or if you have a deep voice but don't work on your movements…you have to work on your weak points. You must give this profession one hundred percent of your time and make sure you study and prepare.

ERNIE HUDSON

Do you think taking drama classes or going to film school would be helpful?

Yes. Absolutely. Whatever situation where you can learn. There are things you don't want to take a chance with. For example, if you know someone who pulls some strings and you get a job on a television show, you're expected to deliver as if you know what you're doing. So, if you haven't taken the time to study or train or learn the basics, you probably will not do a very good job. Word travels very easily. So you need to get prepared, and drama classes and film schools can prepare you. It gives you a chance to be with other people who are doing what you are, and it gives you support. It's a safe environment that gives you time to work on your craft, to learn about stage, direction, and a lot of other little technical things you need to know that will really save you. It's hard to learn all these things on the set because people are not going to take the time as they will in college or workshops.

Did you study with any acting coaches, and what is your advice on acting coaches?

I did for a while, even though I don't remember their names. Most of my studying was through Wayne State University. I then got a scholarship to go to Yale University, where I attended their playwriting program for a year. I have always been a little bit leery of acting coaches, because when I've studied with them I have seen them be brutal and insensitive at times, without realizing the impact that has on some people. I have always received a lot of support for the work I've done, but I have seen other people get blown away and never come back. So acting classes, in my opinion, are not essential. You need to learn and everybody seems to learn in different ways. Some people pick it up better than others. I have always felt that as long as you are working, whatever you don't know you will learn very fast. If you cannot find work, I would recommend workshops. But if you can do a play, even better. It usually won't cost you money, and you will learn much more in a short period of time in front of an audience than you will in a workshop.

How does one obtain representation?

That's a hard one, because it is a real catch-22 situation. If you don't have an agent, you will be asked what you have done, and you probably haven't done much since you don't have an agent. It can become a cycle of running in circles. You really need to make yourself sellable. When I was looking for an agent, I was performing in little theater groups and invited agents to see my work. I sent out announcements which included my pictures and quotes from good reviews. I even called up and pretended to be my own secretary, inviting people down and leaving tickets for them at the door. I was taking the money I made from the show to pay for the tickets—but it helped me to get the agents to come.

You also need photos, but you have to be careful because sometimes they land in the trash basket. But, there may be that one person in a hundred who will look at your picture. You need to try different things because you don't know what's going to stick. The key to it all is persistence.

Can you explain the audition process and how you prepare?

They say they don't want to see a "performance." They call it a "reading," but believe me, it's a performance. You have to do something that will make them look at you differently. Usually when they call you in, you're just one of a group of people. I am now in a position where I may be one of five people.

But what is it about me that is going to get me the job over those other four people? Going in prepared, making things happen, and knowing the material are essential. I like to think about the material—I don't like to get the script in the morning and then audition in the afternoon. I usually need the material overnight to digest it. You may get creative when you force it, but it's still better to know the material and think about the character backwards and forwards. Sometimes you lose a performance just trying to come up with the words. So, be prepared because they do pay attention. Nine out of ten of the other performers did not prepare, so it makes you stand out.

What advice can you give someone who has to work a full-time job while pursuing a career in acting?

Try to take a job that doesn't take you mentally and psychologically on a down trip. You need a job that will give you free time to pursue your acting, so get a job that will give enough money for the basic necessities.

What do you look for when choosing a project?

Now I look for a character that I like or find personally interesting, because every character is a part of yourself. I look for involvement, because I don't like working *for* people; rather, we're doing a movie together, I am in the movie and I am a part of it—not just some guy who comes in and says a few words. So being a part of the whole creative process is very important to me.

What is the most frustrating and then the most gratifying part of being an actor?

The most frustrating is not having people trust me enough to say, "We're doing this project and we would like you to be a part of it." Instead, I have to go in and read, and then wait and see if someone else is available. Then maybe after we do all this they'll decide. That's a very frustrating process.

ERNIE HUDSON

The most gratifying is when you know you've made a contribution—that you actually brought something to your role. That is extremely gratifying to me.

Is it important to live in a city like New York or Los Angeles when first starting out?

It's a lot easier. The media is much broader in New York and Los Angeles. On the other hand, if you are in a city like Minneapolis and there are eight theaters where you can work, that can be especially helpful in the beginning. For some people, it may be important to build your craft in a smaller city and then move to New York or Los Angeles when it's time…and you'll know when that is.

How does one sustain a career?

If you've made a commitment for the long run and work on your weaknesses as I said before, and not limit yourself to certain roles, you should be able to do it all. Try to always bring creativity to the character and understand the rhythm of the character.

At this stage of your career, what are your biggest challenges?

To be able to bring to my work the creativity that I know I can. To have a piece of work I can point to and say, "That's what Ernie Hudson is capable of."

SALLY KELLERMAN

Beautiful Sally Kellerman is probably most remembered for her portrayal of "Hot Lips" Houlihan in Robert Altman's film M*A*S*H, *or as Rodney Dangerfield's vibrant English Professor in* Back to School. *Ms. Kellerman is also a singer and has done several voiceovers for national commercials. Some of her other film credits include* Cousin Cousine, Boris and Natasha, Serial, That's Life, Brewster McCloud, Slither, *and* Loving Couples.

Explain how you started your career.

I went to Hollywood High School, and as a kid I did plays at home. I got my first job from John Morley, who came into the restaurant where I was waitressing. I read for *Enemy of the People.* My first reviews weren't that great, but I continued on. I then did others things...TV, one-liners here and there. I was on *My Three Sons,* and in some feature films...small roles, and live theater...a play called *Call Me By My Rightful Name.* The man who wrote *Psycho,* Joe Stefano, was doing a new series called *Outer Limits.* I got the part of Ingrid, and that is how I really got started. Later, I went on to do *M*A*S*H.* and the rest is history. I've been labeled "hot lips" ever since!

What advice would you give someone considering a career in acting?

I would not get involved unless you have an absolute passion about it and if you really want to do this. You have to give it everything you've got: go to classes, work hard, do plays, study.

How did you maintain a sense of security when faced with rejection?

Rejection is part of the game. The best thing you can do is feel lucky when you do work, because there are five hundred other guys lined up behind you.

Can you recommend acting schools?

I highly recommend Larry Moss, who I have been working with lately. He is wonderful. His studio is called "The Acting Studio" in Santa Monica, California.

SALLY KELLERMAN

What do you look for when choosing a project?

I haven't always had the luxury of choosing projects, so I try to take the best at hand.

What is the most frustrating and then the most gratifying part of being an actress?

The *work* is most gratifying. It's those wonderful, rare times that you get a *director*. Having someone who has a gift with actors is extremely gratifying. The most frustrating for me is when you feel you have a lot to offer and you don't get up to bat.

What suggestions would you give with regard to obtaining representation?

Try to do local plays to be seen. Call agents to come see you.

What advice would you give someone who has to work full-time in another profession while pursuing acting?

Do whatever you can to support yourself by leaving your days free. I was a waitress in a coffee shop. Waitressing in the evenings is always good; it will give you time for auditions during the day.

How do you prepare for an audition?

For me, acting coaches were very important. I always go over my material thoroughly.

At this stage of your career, what are your greatest challenges?

To overcome preconceptions about who one *is* and finding and developing roles that express things that go on in one's life—roles that have meaning. Or...hell, just a good "meaty" role—a good comedy.

Any further advice?

Work at it. Be good at what you do. Develop your talent so you will have something other than just a pretty face. If you really want to be an actor, be prepared for rejection. And most of all, you really need to love this business.

JOEY LAWRENCE

An actor since childhood, Joey's big break came on the long-running series Gimme A Break. *Currently, he has the role of "Joey Russo" on the hit show* Blossom. *In addition to acting, Joey is also a singer. His first album was Number 75 on the "Hot 100" chart. Another shining accomplishment for Joey came when he was voted one of People Magazine's 50 Most Beautiful People.*

How did your career begin?

I started my career at age five doing commercials in New York City. I did fifty or sixty national commercials. I was very lucky because I got a lot of emotional support from my Mom and Dad, which helped me a lot at such a young age. My first pilot project at age five was called *Scamps,* with Bob Denver. At five and three quarter years, Johnny Carson had me on his show. And from that point, I did a show called *Little Shots* and then *Gimme a Break,* where I portrayed the character Joey Donovan for five and a half years. I went on to the series *Blossom,* which I am still doing. I am also a singer, and in 1993 my album went gold worldwide. I am working on a second album.

What advice would you give someone considering a career in acting?

Having a support system is very important. Also you must love it, because you need to give it one hundred and ten percent of your time until it happens. I would also have to stress how essential school is. Don't ever lose track of your education. Getting a college education is very important, because if the acting doesn't work out, you have to have alternatives in the workplace.

JOEY LAWRENCE

What advice can you give someone who has to work full-time in another profession while pursuing his or her acting career?

Acting is a hit-or-miss business. You can be great and talented and you will get that break. Somebody else may be as talented, but may not get that break as quickly. So they will have to get a job, which makes it more difficult because you need time for auditions. You need a job that will give you free time. I know a lot of actors who are waiters and waitresses, which is great because you are dealing with people. A very important part of this business is people skills. Anything else part-time, or a shift job, will give you the time to pursue acting.

How do you prepare for auditions?

Right now in my career I don't have to go through the "cattle call." I am able to bypass sixty or seventy people, for which I am grateful…but it wasn't always like that. You have to go on these auditions with an open mind. Also, it's important to study the character, imagine yourself as the character, and read the material thoroughly.

What do you look for when choosing a project?

Doing *Blossom* makes it difficult for me to choose new projects because of the time factor. This year will probably be my last year on *Blossom,* and I would like to do more dramatic roles—different than my television personality, Joey Russo, who is a very funny, outlandish character.

How does one obtain an agent?

First you need to get professional photographs done, and take them around to different agencies, and try to audition for them. If you have film work on yourself, that would be excellent. Even trying to get in the door using another approach, such as being an assistant to a producer, might help you meet people. There are also books, weekly magazines listing agents and casting agents, and SAG (Screen Actors Guild) offers a list of accredited agents.

At this stage of your career, what are your biggest challenges?

Transferring into the next arena—films and behind the scenes as a director. In the fall, I will be attending USC [University of Southern California]. I have gone from a little boy to a teenager, and now I am eighteen years old—a young adult—and that is a category type I will be pursuing.

Any further advice?

You need to have a support system, especially when you are young. You are in an adult world and you are a child, so for me, my Mom and Dad gave me the greatest thing: support. They shielded me, and without them it would have been very tough. Now I feel I can handle it. But for a young person, a support system is so essential. I would also have to say if you really want to do this, you have to sacrifice some things for your dream. The financial rewards of this profession can be great, but in the beginning you may not be able to accept a high-paying job and pursue this profession. So, sacrifices definitely need to be made. Most important, you must love it and be willing to give it all of your time and dedication.

KATHY NAJIMY

Kathy was known to New York audiences as one half of "The Kathy and Mo Show," which she created with Mo Gaffney and starred in, off Broadway, for a year and a half. Her feature film credits include The Fisher King *and* Hocus Pocus. *She is probably most remembered for her role as the singing nun in* Sister Act *and* Sister Act 2.

Would you explain how you got started in your career?

I've always been prone to acting, since the second grade. That is how I realized to be creative in a real outward sense. I started out doing some acting in San Diego. I was pretty much undercover. I was the kind of actress who got cast in things her friends insisted to the director to put me in. I wasn't cast a lot. Then I did some musicals. I had the parts which I call the "Ethel Mertz parts." I always played the friend.

From there I did political theatre, a group called "Sisters on Stage," for five years. It was the first, other than my one-woman show, that I could combine my politics and my acting. I then did some more legitimate theatre and met Mo Gaffney. We wrote "The Kathy and Mo Show." The show took off and we moved it to New York, where we did small cabaret, small off Broadway, and a big off Broadway for a year and a half. From "Kathy and Mo" is where I got the attention for films. My first film was *The Fisher King*, but *Sister Act* was my biggest role where I took off and got the most visibility.

Is it important to live in a city like New York or Los Angeles when first starting out?

I did it all the wrong way, but it worked for me. Some people need to feel confident, so they stay in their small towns until they achieve the kind of things that give them enough confidence to go on to New York or Los Angeles. I personally got no attention in my hometown. It took for me to move to New York to get attention, which is funny because it's a much more difficult place. It's also the taste of the town and environment. The environment was right for the kind of thing we were doing with "The Kathy and Mo Show." It was hip to be political. Lily Tomlin was on Broadway doing really great; Whoopi Goldberg had already done her one-woman show. The atmosphere was ripe. It was being in the right place at the right time. I realized I wasn't doing anything different than the last ten years—it's just that nobody paid attention.

KATHY NAJIMY

I would still say go with what your soul tells you to do. Some people feel stifled and need to go to a city like New York or Los Angeles. For me, I just needed to get out, so New York worked for me. Also, luck has a lot to do with it. My one big advice, though, don't wait! As performers, we're taught someone else is smarter than us out there, that we need to catch their attention because they have better taste than we do. They need to pluck us out of somewhere and put us somewhere, and that's true for a lot of people that are thin and blonde or have relatives in the business. But for the rest of us, that's probably not going to happen. So what you need to do is decide that you have the best judgment and decide what you want, and make it happen, wherever that may be.

How does one obtain an agent?

When I was doing "The Kathy and Mo Show," the first time off Broadway was in a little ninety-seat house called "The Second Stage." The two women who run it, Carol Rothman and Robin Goodman, called their friend Sam Cohn, who is a mega-agent at ICM. We lucked out and he came to see the show. I called him the next day. I had to call about a hundred times to get him on the line. So getting back to how one obtains an agent, you must be AGGRESSIVE and PERSISTENT, with capital letters. You can't think one call or one letter is going to capture someone's attention in Hollywood, which is so "MTV-fleeting" that you need to be persistent. Who cares if you're a pest? You're not going to date them—you're just going to work with them.

I finally did get Sam Cohn on the phone and we had a meeting. I did not know any protocol at that time, so I just came out and asked, "Do you want to sign us?" He asked if we wanted to be signed, and of course my reply was "yes." So we were signed early on, around 1986. He has been my agent ever since. Another way is to invite people to come see you. Don't be discouraged, because a hundred of them will turn you down. Even though that did not happen to me, it's happened to a lot of people I know. Eventually one of those people will come see you.

How did you deal with rejection?

By inventing something else for me to do. Rejection never really goes away. I feel bad for the day, scream and throw things, and then the next day get on to something else.

How do you prepare for auditions?

I'm really awful in auditions, which is why I love getting offered things. What I really learned is being unprepared just means you're really scared. So if you don't get it, you can have an excuse—that you weren't prepared. The hardest thing for me to get over is that I have to prepare. And if I don't get it, it's because I didn't get it—not because I have a ready-made excuse. So I would encourage people to prepare.

What advice would you give someone who has to work full-time in another job while pursuing an acting career?

I haven't had to do that a whole lot, although I was an operator for AT&T in San Diego for eight years. I would have to say to get something flexible that will give you free time for auditions. The ideal thing would be to hit a good horse at the races!

What do you look for when choosing a project?

Right now I'm at a particular phase where I've had to turn down a lot of work. That's very scary for someone who grew up on welfare. Every six months it's different—it just depends on what I've done. I just finished three funny movies, *Sister Act, Hocus Pocus* and *Sister Act 2,* which gained a lot of attention. People know me from that, which is fine, but now it's my responsibility to make sure they don't only know me for that. For my very next project that is released nationwide, it needs to be very different. You don't want to be typecast. It's all really the timing.

How does one sustain a career?

I don't know that one can. I feel secure in the fact that I am a director and writer—that's what I did before I acted and I am still writing and directing. For me, I enjoy doing those things as much as acting. You need control of your own career. If you're scared and waiting and betting your self-esteem on whether you get a part, then "bye-bye." Don't wait—take control.

At this stage of your career, what are your biggest challenges?

I think my biggest challenge is to do something different from how people know me, and pull it off successfully.

Any further advice?

Please don't take it seriously—Hollywood is a game. Like playing Monopoly, you start at start and you roll the dice and do your best to be the smartest you can be. If you have to go back to start and roll the dice again, it's okay. Don't let it impact who you are in your mind or your heart.

MICHAEL NOURI

Michael made his screen debut as Ali MacGraw's boyfriend in the film Goodbye Columbus. *Some of his other film credits include* Flashdance, Imagemaker, *and* The Hidden. *His television credits include the series* Beacon Hill, The Gangster Chronicles, Bay City Blues, *and* Love and War. *He has also appeared in the television movies* Changes, Quiet Victory, In the Arms of a Killer, Shattered Dreams, *and the mini-series* The Last Convertible.

How did you begin your career?

When I was fifteen years old, I was going to an all-boys boarding school in Connecticut and was cast as the judge in Gilbert and Sullivan's *Trial By Jury.* In college I acted in productions that included Harold Pinter's *The Birthday Party, The Fantastiks,* and *Who's Afraid of Virginia Woolf?*

In 1967 I made my first trip to Los Angeles. I lied my way into an agent's (Freddy Fields) office, and was sent over to Paramount Studios to meet with Larry Pierce who was directing a movie called *Goodbye Columbus,* starring unknowns Ali McGraw and Richard Benjamin. I was cast in the role of Ali's boyfriend. I had never been in front of a movie camera and I was terrified! Mercifully, I had very little to say or do and managed to get by. This proved to be a very valuable lesson in that I learned that it takes more than bravado to make an actor. I had yet to learn how to turn self-consciousness into concentration. I was like a plumber or a carpenter with no tools, or a public speaker without his pants. Never again! It was at this time I enrolled in an acting class with my first teacher, Lee Stasberg.

My next gig was waiting tables until I got a Broadway play produced by David Merrick, called *Forty Carats,* directed by Abe Burrows and starring Julie Harris. Acting with Julie Harris will always be one of the highlights of my career. Just watching her prepare and rehearse was a lesson in acting. Of course, her performance was great—like a Rolls Royce fresh out of the factory. But

MICHAEL NOURI

witnessing what went into creating and crafting the end product was, to me, the true marvel: [the] gradual paring away of all the "clay" that has nothing to do with the final "sculpture"—the character. I was witnessing the greatest acting lesson of all, that cannot be taught in any class: the power and inspiration and generosity of an artist doing what she loves most in life. I pay homage to Julie Harris, whose example taught me the value of concentration, dedication to detail, generosity of spirit toward all fellow workers, and the infectious, childlike excitement that comes with doing what you love to do, when you do it with love.

How do you maintain a sense of security when faced with rejection?

I think the real question is how to maintain confidence when you're not chosen for a role after you've put everything you've got into preparing for an audition. The answer is to keep working, because only through working can you know and trust your instrument and discover what your unique truth—your "voice"—is. When an actor comes from his or her passion and doesn't get a role, there is no sense of rejection. It is the employer's loss, not the actor's.

Tell us more about your formal training in acting or film schools.

I have studied with Lee Strasberg, William Alderson, Robert Arodica, Sandy Meisner and Stella Adler and Larry Moss. My teachers extend to every dedicated actor and actress I work with or watch. My greatest teachers are life itself and, of course, human behavior.

What do you look for when choosing a project?

It's always wonderful if you find a piece of material that says something about humanity. Stella Alder emphasized this by saying, "What the actor does for the theater is the truth...blood. It's quality, it's theater with a big 'T.' The theater will give you an understanding of life and will educate you. Your profession gives you some kind of idea in living up to your potential, living up to your mind, living up to your total self." I can't improve on that. I look for an idea that will elevate my life and challenge my way of thinking and perceiving.

How do you prepare yourself for auditions?

I tell myself that I am going to tell the truth from my character's point of view to the people in that room—and tell this truth with all the passion in my being.

What is the most frustrating and then the most gratifying part of being an actor?

The most frustrating aspect is being perceived in terms of type and appearance, rather than by substance and ability. The gratification lies in being hired for who you specifically are and for what you can bring to a role.

What suggestions can you give with regard to obtaining representation?

The proverbial "catch-22": to get a job, you need an agent; to get an agent, you need a job. A very curious phenomenon. I think it serves a very useful purpose because from the get-go, if you are not really passionate about doing it, you are going to fail as soon as it gets hard. For the long run, talent and hard work will always be acknowledged. It's a matter of being patient, persistent, and passionate. Also, it doesn't hurt to be thick-skinned. The trick is to drop the armor and to be completely porous and vulnerable when onstage or in front of the camera.

At this stage of your career, what are your greatest challenges?

Practicing everything I have been talking about. Also to stay out of competition and comparison with fellow actors. To be true to what I do know, and to let myself be excited about what I have yet to learn. And to not be lazy. It's like a relationship: when you're in love, it all works, but to stay in love, you have to choose to do the work. Now there's a challenge!

What further advice could you give someone just starting out?

Work as much as possible in projects and material you believe in. Don't get into the business to be a movie star or for the money, because stardom will come and go, money will come and go. Only get involved for the love of it, and with the absolute confidence that in this, the toughest of all professions, are held some of the greatest teachings about life and humanity. And to have fun! Because when all is said and done, people pay to see us play.

SARAH JESSICA PARKER

Sarah appeared in her first TV special, The Little Match Girl, *at age eight. A part in an off-Broadway play led to a two-year Broadway run in the lead role of* Annie. *She gained national recognition with her starring role in the television series* Square Pegs, *followed by* A Year In The Life *and in the TV movie* The Ryan White Story, *among others. Her film credits include* Footloose, Girls Just Want To Have Fun, Flight Of The Navigator, L.A. Story, Honeymoon In Vegas, *and* Hocus Pocus.

Explain how you began your career.

I'm from Cincinnati, Ohio. There are eight kids in my family. When I was growing up, art was a fundamental part of our lives. The city where I lived was fairly small, but it was known for its cultural contributions. And a lot of the programs were free for kids, which was great, because we did not have a lot of money. So we naturally developed an interest in the various aspects of the arts.

When I was eight years old I saw an ad in the paper and auditioned for Hans Christian Anderson's *The Little Match Girl.* There was no real reason that I auditioned, but out of the five-hundred little girls that auditioned, I got the part. The people were incredibly wonderful. I had a great time doing it and found it to be educational in certain ways.

I then decided to pursue acting locally in Cincinnati. In another newspaper ad, I saw that Harold Pinter was looking for two young people to be leads in a play going to Broadway. *The Turn of the Screw* by Henry James had been adapted for the stage and called *The Innocence*, with Claire Bloom playing the governess. My brother and I auditioned and got parts.

My family then decided to move to New York for lots of different reasons; the focus was not on my brother and me. My father wanted to, and did, start up a business there. We had an agent in New York and, because we'd been seen in the Broadway play, he sent us out to a lot of auditions and we got a great deal of work. When you are young with naive luck, nothing really matters; you have nothing at stake and you are not dependent on acting for income. Everything is easy. I worked a lot and did a lot of theater, and that's basically how I got started.

SARAH JESSICA PARKER

Did you have any formal training?

No, I didn't—and I still don't. I don't encourage that, but I was always working and that was my training.

Since you started early, do you have any advice for young people starting out?

Always check with the unions to see if agents are legitimate. If someone says that you have to pay them to be your agent, that is illegal. The best way to learn is to study and read plays. There are creative dramatic programs locally in different cities. There are a lot of play readings. Bigger cities tend to have a lot of cultural activities for young people, and those are invaluable. It doesn't matter where you live. Small theater groups are very educational.

The reason I suggest reading plays is that it gives you a chance to practice your reading, which is very important. Read plays with your friends for practice. Visiting museums and seeing plays is always educational. Acting classes and modeling classes are not the only way to learn.

I think finishing school and an education are vital before you seriously pursue a career in the entertainment industry. I don't endorse young people working, even though I did. If you are good and talented, you will work eventually. One of my big regrets was that I was out of school a lot.

Did you finish school?

Yes, but I was so distracted by my lifestyle, that it was difficult. I think it is so important to interact with young, "normal" people your own age—more important than being a movie star.

How did you maintain a sense of security when faced with rejection?

I don't think I did. In all honesty, I am as insecure and have as many deep-seated neuroses as anybody else. I don't think that ever changes. You are a human being and human beings react to being rejected. You can't shut that feeling off. I think what's best to do is to develop a bit of perspective—you can't do that right away. When you are young, it doesn't matter as much. When acting is your sole means of making a living, the values change—everything means more. The stakes are incredibly high, so that when somebody doesn't want you, you cannot help but hurt a little bit.

There are a lot of legitimate reasons for being rejected. For example, I met with a director. It seemed like a perfectly good meeting. I liked him and he liked me, but he didn't want me for the part. I wasn't right for it. That's completely valid. In his mind I wasn't right and there was nothing I could do about it. It's perfectly all right, but that doesn't mean that it doesn't hurt. My theory is to try to be magnanimous and philosophical. It's not about any "spiritual path"—it's the only way to survive. We all rationalize to get through life. If we weren't able to, we'd all be dead or suicidal—in any business, not just acting. So you have to learn to develop perspective, and that takes time. In three or four years you'll be less depressed if you don't get a particular job.

How do you prepare for auditions?

I have no particular way. I just work on the material to be really prepared.

How do you get an agent?

Finding an agent is very difficult: agents have so many clients and not enough work. I'd say join small theater groups and invite agents to come to see you perform. In New York there's a paper called *Backstage* where all open calls are listed and you don't have to be a member of a union or have an agent. It's rough because you have to stand in line very early in the morning and take a number—but sometimes that is the best way. Other than that, just keep looking for your own work.

What suggestions would you give to someone who has to work a full-time job while pursuing an acting career?

Try to find a job that is accommodating to pursuing your goal. Working nights may be a good idea. I know a lot of people who work as waiters or waitresses in the evenings, which leaves their days free to go to auditions.

What is the most frustrating and then the most gratifying part of being an actress?

The most frustrating thing is not having control. In other professions you have more control. For example, if I had chosen to be a writer, I could write twenty-four hours a day—I can't act in my own bedroom.

The great thing about having a little success is that you have more options, more opportunities...you have a little more control. Not having control is hard because you need someone to tell you what you are allowed to do—and until you're allowed, you can't do it. That's the most frustrating part.

The most gratifying part is the recognition you get from your fans. When people respond to you on the street it is a completely wonderful, lovely feeling. I find it very pleasant and not bothersome at all. It's very gratifying.

SARAH JESSICA PARKER

Having done both television and film, could you explain the differences between the two?

Television tends to be a lot more "condensed." The beauty of doing a series, given that it's really fast and really hard work, is that it's a long commitment—nine months or so. The character really gets a life every week. It's a new experience. The character gets to change and grow and learn and you get to play all these wonderful emotions.

The beauty of film is that your schedule is more generous. You really get to figure out what your character is all about in the story. You can work on every little moment because time allows that.

I like both, because both are helpful in creating character. With television, it's like a viewmaster: you keep going and going. With film, it's like putting a microscope on a character.

What do you look for when choosing a project?

I always look for things that I can "telescope" and say: "Will I regret this in ten years?" I try to do things I feel "one-hundred-percent-good" about. I'm very lucky because I've always worked with incredible people—in film, television and theater.

I always try to pick things that are quality. There have been many times that I've chosen to do a play rather than television or film. It may seem sort of mad, but at the time it was the right thing to do. I look for the opportunity to work with good people, new text, and a new challenge.

What are your greatest challenges?

Finding better roles and continuing to work with great actors and directors—that's truly the way to grow and what I continue to look for.

JOE PENNY

One of television's top romantic men, Joe Penny most recently starred in Terror in the Night *on CBS Television. In 1981, he starred as the infamous mobster Bugsy Siegel, in NBC-TV's* The Gangster Chronicles. *In 1984, Mr. Penny starred as "Nick Ryder" on NBC's successful* Riptide, *a mid-season replacement which ran for two and a half years. For five seasons, he costarred in* Jake and the Fatman *with the late William Conrad. Other credits to his name include two CBS Television movies with Lisa Hartman:* Roses Are for the Rich *and* The Operation; *costarring roles in an NBC* Perry Mason *TV movie and a two-hour* Matlock; *and the critically acclaimed NBC special* Blood Vows: The Story of a Mafia Wife, *with Melissa Gilbert. The multi-talented actor also costarred in several feature films:* Our Winning Season, Gangster Wars I and II, S.O.B., *and* Happy Birthday.

Would you explain how you got started in your career?

It just happened. I did not grow up wanting to be an actor, nor did I grow up in a show business family. I did, however, grow up with television and was a television baby in the '60s and '70s, when television was exploring.

My career began one night as I was picking up a friend from his acting class. The class ran late, so I sat down and watched. I had no idea what was going on except that I saw a group of people expressing themselves, seeming to have fun. After the class, the teacher approached me and asked if I had any interest in participating. At the time, I said "no." Four or five days passed and I decided to try it...that's when everything happened. I took classes from Joan Darling, Lee Strasberg, Charles Conrad, Stella Adler, Vincent Chase, and Sandy Meisner. I still study acting now.

How did you maintain a sense of security in the face of rejection?

In the beginning, rejection made me try harder...it motivated me and it actually made me angry. If you don't want to be judged, rejected, ridiculed, talked about, or put up on the auction block, you should not be in this business as an actor.

JOE PENNY

What do you look for when choosing a project?

It happens creatively. For example, you see a person and for some unknown reason, that person catches your eye. It's called chemistry, and its the same way with a script. It makes my heart pound. A good script is hard to put down. I know it's good if I can't put it down...if I want to inhale it. That's how I know if I want to pursue the project. My first instinct is usually correct; the second one is usually fear of following the first.

Have you done film work?

Yes, I did *Gangster Wars, Parts 1 and 2*—from the mini-series *Gangster Chronicles*—for foreign release. I also did a film with Dennis Quaid and Scott Jacoby called *Our Winning Season.* The most interesting film I've done was *S.O.B. S.O.B.* was a Blake Edwards film—a take-off on Hollywood. I got the chance to work with some great people and to befriend a great actor, William Holden. That was one of the greatest moments of my life.

What is the difference between television and film work?

With film, there's a bigger budget. It's slower paced and a lot of waiting around. With television, it's a much faster pace. Television eats material. Also in television, you do anywhere from thirty-five to forty-five set-ups a day. On a film, they'll do ten to twelve set-ups a day. I think there is more television product out than good feature product. The reason why people become addicted to a television series is because, for the most part, they are not hard to watch. The cast is very clean, very "in and out." You know what they are about. And maybe they don't get critical acclaim, but they stay on for five to six years or so. Also, with regard to feature, why would people want to go out and spend $7.50 on a ticket when they can watch a good television show and not have to think or struggle just to be entertained?

What advice would you give to a person who has to work at a full-time job in another profession while pursuing his or her acting career?

I don't think you can have a full-time job and pursue acting part-time. It really depends on how serious you are...you have to want to eat, breath and sleep with this career. I worked part-time jobs during the day and went to acting class at night, but my number-one priority was always to be in acting class, so I tried to get a job that allowed me free time for class.

What is the most frustrating and then the most gratifying part of being an actor?

The most gratifying for me, is to take something off a page and do it and have someone else really connect with what you are doing. It's also the highest high to be acknowledged by your peers. As far as the most frustrating aspect of acting, it's *all* frustrating—particularly in the beginning!

How do you prepare for auditions?

I break down the script to make sure that it's right to prepare for the part. The most important thing is working with my acting coaches.

What suggestions can you give with regards to obtaining representation?

First, try to find an agent who will give you the opportunity to do an audition piece, if you don't already have any film of yourself. The Screen Actors Guild has a list of accredited agents. I also had eight-by-ten photos that I would leave with agents. What you really need is perseverance.

Express the importance of living in a city like New York or Los Angeles when first starting out.

You have to be where the action is if you want to be in this business. In New York you have theater. In Los Angeles you have television and film.

At this stage of your career, what are your greatest challenges?

My greatest challenges are ahead of me—when they present themselves, I'll let you know.

What additional advice would you give an aspiring actor?

If you want to be an actor, to be a star, or make a lot of money, those are the wrong reasons. If you do it because you love it and it's in your heart, then stay the course. Your dream will come if you love your craft. There is a quote which reads, "Love the art within yourself, not yourself within the art."

KELLY PRESTON

Kelly Preston is one of the more splendid young actresses gracing today's Hollywood. Born in Hawaii, Kelly studied drama first at USC, and then at UCLA. Her first professional acting was in daytime soap operas, while still an undergraduate. She then became a regular on the television series For Love and Honor, *performed other television roles, and went on to feature films, including* Secret Admirer, 52 Pick Up, Twins, Mischief, *and* Experts, *where she met her husband, John Travolta.*

How did you get started in your acting career?

I was living in Hawaii, where I was born and raised. I met a photographer who wanted to take pictures. From there, I did a lot of Japanese print work and commercials, and then several American national commercials. I was then able to get my Screen Actors Guild card. I then moved to Los Angeles, where I got an agent. My first audition was for a soap opera, which I ended up getting.

Did formal education or training have a bearing on what you do today?

I studied theater and took several technical classes at USC and UCLA. When I left college, I studied with several acting teachers, including Milton Kasalas and Gordon Hunt. I had the freedom to explore myself as an actress and work on a variety of different roles and characters. For me, it was hooking up with the right teacher or the most supportive improvisation group. Training can be helpful as long as the classes don't get into heavy evaluation and invalidation. Sometimes, safe and healthy learning places are hard to find.

What advice would you give someone considering a career in acting?

As long as you believe this is what you truly want, and you can't be happy doing anything else, then by all means pursue it. Acting can be gloriously rewarding, and yet sometimes painful. Don't take the rejection personally. Read William Goldman's *Adventures in the Screen Trade.*

KELLY PRESTON

Do you have to live in New York or L.A. when first starting your career?

There are more opportunities in the larger cities, but I would not discount the smaller cities, especially when just starting. A lot of times, the smaller cities have small productions or wonderful repertory companies. Films and commercials will often search in the smaller cities for undiscovered talent. But, for the greatest number of opportunities I would recommend Los Angeles, New York, or Chicago.

What advice would you give someone who has to work full-time in another profession while pursuing his or her career in acting?

I believe two different theories regarding this question. First, I think it's very difficult for a person who has to work full-time in another profession while pursuing acting. Acting takes a lot of your time. You must be able to take time off if you get the job. It's also good to exercise creatively. Take dance and voice classes. On the other hand, if this is your dream, then by all means working in another profession can also be helpful. It can keep you extroverted and in touch with something other than acting. You can meet interesting people. It's also helpful to be involved in something else so you can keep your mind off of the waiting game—waiting to see if you got the part!

Can you recommend any acting teachers?

I have studied with Gordon Hunt, Bill Sorrells, Jered Barclay, and Milton Kasalas. They are all excellent teachers.

How do you prepare yourself for auditions?

I read the script to get a feel of the whole piece and how my character fits into it. I read the audition scenes over and over to extract every bit of information. Then I memorize all of the lines in those scenes. This is contrary to what some people believe. I've heard it said "If you don't memorize it and if you work with the script still in your hand, the director will think that this is only a work in progress and that you can really do much better." I think looking up and down from a script can be distracting and lead to an unfocused performance and should only be done if it's a cold reading.

Is there anything specific that you look for when choosing a project?

There are several elements I consider regarding a project. For me, the script, my character, and the director are the most important elements. Usually, a talented director can make a less than interesting script seem quite interesting. Also, the other actors who are cast can make a project more inviting.

How do you maintain a sense of security in the face of rejection?

I don't take it personally! It's as simple as that. It's amazing, when you understand the process involved with casting a film. Recently, I was able to stop behind the scenes in a casting session. What I learned surprised me. Out of all the women who auditioned, there were six women who would have been wonderful in the role. The reason they chose the actress they did was something very specific in regards to the other actors already cast. There are so many different reasons why an actor is cast or not. So it's really important to not take it personally, unless you feel you have given a bad audition. If that's the case, don't worry about it. Try to do better next time.

Why did you become an actress?

It's the only profession that I was drawn to, where I am really happy to go to work every day. I look forward to working on each new project. It's very fulfilling creatively, and often you meet some wonderful people.

How does one sustain a career as an actor or an actress?

Try to play as wide a variety of characters as possible and stretch as an actor. That will keep you fulfilled and interested. Don't compromise your own personal integrity, and don't burn your bridges. Try to keep enjoying yourself.

What is the most frustrating and then the most gratifying part of being an actress?

The most gratifying part of being an actress is winning a great and creatively satisfying role, and then feeling as though you have given a fulfilling performance. And to be honest, the salary is terrific and the work is enjoyable. One of the most frustrating things is the "hurry-up-and-wait syndrome." There is often a lot of time between scenes when you are waiting to perform, and you feel as though you are being paid to wait. Another frustrating thing is that there are a shortage of really good roles and so many talented actresses to fill them.

What is the difference between television and film work?

The shooting pace in television is usually a lot quicker. If you are on a series, it's steady work throughout the year, with a few months on hiatus. Sometimes, you will find exquisitely written pieces by respected playwrights on some of the cable stations (PBS, TNT, etc.). With film, you tend to have a lot more time to rehearse and explore the character. Each film is a complete entity and a wonderful experience with a new group of people and a chance to explore a new character. Your personal life tends to be a lot more flexible with a lot more time off.

ALAN RACHINS

As attorney Douglas Brackman on the hit NBC series L.A. Law, *Alan Rachins created a complex character whose bottom-line professionalism was balanced by the human comedy of his personal life. Alan earned both Golden Globe and Emmy nominations for his portrayal of Attorney Brackman. He has also performed in a succession of plays, including the original Broadway production of* After the Rain *and* Hadrian the Seventh. *In addition, he has appeared in the Jackie Collins mini-series entitled,* Lady Boss, *as well as NBC's Perry Mason mystery:* The Case of the Silent Singer *and several other starring roles in television movies of the week. His other credits include such feature films as Henry Jaglom's* Always, *and* Heart Condition, *with Denzel Washington and Bob Hoskins.*

How did you get started in your career?

First it started with the fantasy of wanting to do this and loving movies. I was hooked since eighth grade, when I saw James Dean in *Rebel Without A Cause.* Sitting in that dark theater next to my father, something clicked. I was eleven years old. My mother had died the previous month after a long illness. All kinds of emotions were tangled up inside. Among them: anger at my dad. When James Dean yelled at his father, it was thrilling. I knew I had to be an actor.

I left college after two and a half years. I was in a business school, the Wharton School of Finance, and just went to New York without knowing anyone or having any idea of what to do. I just started looking for people to study with. I got most of my information from a trade magazine, *Backstage.* It had ads for acting teachers, auditions, photographers.

I went to The Circle in the Square Theater School for three months. Then I started going to auditions. Over the years I continued to take classes. Among my favorite teachers were Uta Hagen, William Ball, then Warren Robertson and Phillip Burton (who was Richard Burton's stepfather). Then in Los Angeles I studied with Kim Stanley and comedy improvisation with Harvey Lembeck. They were great. Harvey has passed away, but the class continues in the capable hands of his son and daughter.

ALAN RACHINS

Do you have to live in New York or L.A. when starting your career?

It's hard to know. Everyone does things differently. New York was definitely the place for me to go; there was a lot of theater to do. I think you should be in a place where you can make safe mistakes. I started in summer stock building sets, cleaning toilets, doing workshops in small theaters, and trying to get agents to come to see me when they couldn't have cared less! I think it's smarter for most people to get substantial stage experience before trying for work in film and television.

What suggestions can you give with regard to obtaining representation?

You need some experience, whether it be in dinner theater out of town, or showcases in a big city. You have to be where you can do something. Then, keep contacting agents. Get them to come see you work. If they don't come, follow up with them. Let them know your reviews. Get to know people. Let them know that you exist. Tell them what you are doing. Tell them who you are studying with. Prepare a terrific audition scene that you can do in an agent's office. Be assertive in asking them to let you perform it.

What is the most frustrating and then the most gratifying part of being an actor?

The most frustrating thing is when you are trying to get representation...trying to get yourself into something to show yourself off. You keep trying to get better...trying to find the right class for you. The most gratifying is when you have been good in something....when you have had the opportunity to do something and you really felt satisfied that you were good in it.

What do you look for when choosing a project?

Well, I'm not exactly in the position to choose. I can choose not to do a project. When a part comes my way, I look to see if it's a part I haven't done before, or just whether or not I think I'd be good at it. Frankly, you weigh all the factors: who are the people involved, the quality of the project, the part, the money, and because of family considerations, the location and the demands on your time. And again: the part.

Why did you decide to do the "Brackman" character on **L.A. Law?**

Because they asked me. And for that, I knock wood. I dance for joy and consider myself to be fortunate. I also loved the character. He was a character that I could have been had I gone into my father's business, because he (Brackman) went into his father's business and had a dominating father. I went to business school and my father wanted me to go into his business. But I chose a different road. It's sort of like I walked down the same road as Brackman, except that I had the guts to get out and say that I wanted to go into show business. Beside being able to link into the character emotionally, I'm lucky that *L.A. Law* had wonderful writers who developed many sides of the Brackman character which kept it challenging, surprising, and fun. I also loved the fact that the character got to play both dramatic scenes and comedic situations.

How do you maintain a sense of security when faced with rejection?

I have said horrible things at home about the people who have rejected me and I feel incredibly sorry for their lack of vision and taste! I wish them well and hope they will develop better abilities along the way. Then you look at yourself to see what it is about you that missed. Is it the next acting class or kind of therapy or is it something that's going to juice you up and make you better? I also try to look at where I went wrong—did I give a bad reading, did I give a poor interview?

How do you prepare for auditions?

You go to a lot of acting classes and feel comfortable with yourself and the material. If I do well with the material, then I think I have a really good shot at this. And if I don't, then we are both better off going in a different direction.

What advice would you give aspiring actors who also have to maintain a full-time job?

Whatever allows them the opportunity to go to an acting class and to auditions. Do whatever it is that will get you the money to cover your life so you can live and also takes care of your acting classes and auditions.

Do you still find it necessary to take classes?

If a part were to come along that was different, or I hadn't done it before...if the part had something to offer, I would take classes. I generally overprepare.

What is the difference between film and television work?

I don't see a big difference from what I have done so far.

ALAN RACHINS

What advice would you give an aspiring actor?

First, good preparation before you jump in is very important, because people will remember their first impressions of you. If you are not ready, people cannot see inside of you. They will not see the greatness that you have inside. They will only see what you are showing them, so you have to be ready to have it to show. I wish I had gone to one of those two-year acting schools in New York before I started to audition. I started auditioning right away, long before I was prepared, and I gave enormous numbers of horrible auditions. It would have been smarter to have avoided that.

What are your opinions of film schools?

I also went to a film school. I went to The American Film Institute for two years. It helped me as an actor because you see yourself as part of the process. And there are a lot of actors who come from theater who are very resistant to the stopping and starting of filmmaking, and they have a lot of difficulty. I think film school, for me, has made me kind of friendly with the equipment (camera, etc.), and I feel comfortable in the environment. It took away a lot of the mystique, the fear of the camera, etc. So it was helpful in that way. I also went to film school after I had been an actor in New York for ten years and felt I wasn't getting anywhere quick enough. I decided to explore writing and directing, and that is when I went to A.F.I. I've written scripts for episodic television, as well as directed, and hope to do more in the future.

Do you find it hard to sustain a career as an actor?

I don't know—it remains to be seen. But in starting out (and it took twenty-five years to get *L.A. Law*), I went through a number of phases where I was fed up. I thought that I wanted to give up...I couldn't do it anymore. I went to a job counselor once or twice. There comes a certain point, however, when you don't have enough education in your background and the job counselor says that she doesn't really know what else you can do. Then, you take a deep breath and say that you'll give it another try. I did take time off to finish my B.A. at Empire State College. It's a wonderful program in The State University of New York that encourages independent study and allows participation in designing your own curriculum.

Is it gratifying when people ask you for your autograph?

It's great! I came from a small town (Brookline, Massachusetts), then I went to New York and it was a nightmare! No one knew me in New York. You go into the bank, but the tellers keep changing and you remain a stranger. You go into the same little neighborhood grocery store, but the people who run it are too afraid to smile and you remain a stranger. People don't smile in New York. They don't act like they recognize you. It's horrible. You are totally anonymous in a city like New York, especially when you come from a small town where everyone knows you. I'd say that ninety-nine percent of the time, it's delightful and terrific! I love it! The audience response is terrific! Once, in a yogurt store, a guy handed me a portable phone: "My wife is a fan. Could you say 'hello' to her?" We had a nice talk.

At this stage of your career, what are your greatest challenges?

I'm a little embarrassed about going through a whole list of dreams that I have not yet fulfilled. I have a lot of things that I want to do, and I hope I just get the opportunity to do them. Some people can look at being in a TV series like *L.A. Law* as a pinnacle of what you have reached. Or, it can be like an entry-level position and you can go from there. It depends how it works out. I'm hoping and looking at it as an entry-level position and wanting to move well beyond it.

ERIC ROBERTS

Eric Roberts started his career doing children's plays throughout Atlanta. Since then, Eric has explored a wide variety of roles in such films as Star 80, The Coca Cola Kid, The Pope of Greenwich Village, Runaway Train, King of the Gypsies, *and* Final Analysis. *Recently, he just completed a film entitled* The Specialist, *with Sylvester Stallone and Sharon Stone. He is the brother of Julia Roberts.*

How did your career begin?

The seeds of my career were planted in my childhood. My father had a company called "The Actors and Writers Workshop," funded by The Martin Luther King Foundation. We had a show-mobile and performed children's plays throughout Atlanta. We'd tour the underprivileged areas during the week, and do theater in the park on the weekends, much like Joe Papp's public theater in Central Park in Manhattan. I acted in most of the productions and took the work very seriously. My father was my original teacher. His encouragement has remained very significant in my life.

I then attended a summer session at the Royal Academy of Dramatic Art in London. After that, I was accepted and studied at the American Academy. I was not invited back to the American Academy, however. (It must have been at least mildly amusing to watch certain careers flourish for certain people they dismissed.)

Does an aspiring actor have to live in New York or Los Angeles when first starting out?

Unfortunately it is important to live in New York or Los Angeles when starting a career as an actor. I'd recommend New York. These days there is a lot of television and some film production also happening in Chicago, Vancouver, Toronto, Atlanta, Miami, and other major cities. There is local theater all over the place. But there is still more to be learned, exposed to, etc., in New York or Los Angeles.

What advice would you give to someone who has to work full-time in another profession while pursuing acting?

I think it can be very important to maintain a full-time job while pursuing an acting career, because having your income taken care of lends peace of mind. Every free hour should be devot-

ERIC ROBERTS

ed to classes or auditions, or reading *Drama-logue* or the trade papers such as *Variety, Hollywood Reporter,* or rehearsing a theatrical production or a scene for class. Persistence in attitude pays off, even if it feels like you're just spinning your wheels.

Explain how to prepare for an audition.

As soon as you hear that you have an audition you should make it your business to get as much material as you can. Try to read the whole script, not just the sides. Get two copies of the sides so that you can run the scene with someone you trust after you've worked on it by yourself. I believe in doing the free-associative, emotional work and then beginning to focus on the material.

Get really comfortable with the material. If you run it a thousand times, on the nine-hundred and ninety-fifth time you may find something new and totally unique that may earn you the role. If it's deadly serious, dramatic material, find a place for humor. If it's comedy, find a place to take the absurd, scripted circumstances deathly seriously. Go through the audition finally simulating the conditions under which you may actually walk in the room where all the producers, casting people, and directors are. Do everything you can to insulate yourself and to enjoy the work and to be your most accessible, focused, and as relaxed as possible. Even if memorization is not required, memorize.

Can you explain the difference between television and film work?

Television shoots X-amount of film in eight or eighteen days, where film will shoot the exact same amount in twenty or fifty-five days. Television pays the most attention to being sure that things run smoothly and on schedule. Technically, time spent between director and actors on character interaction is considered a luxury, though everyone tries to make this happen. If a film has a small budget, it can be much like trying to shoot something for television. If the budget is more substantial, there is time afforded for detail and really creating something. In film, the choices are generally bolder and not designed to please everybody. Television seems to deal with topical issues perhaps more than film does, but it gives everything a much more superficial treatment.

When faced with rejection, how did you maintain a sense of security?

I was very lucky and spent most of the beginning of my career getting most of the roles I auditioned for, and being asked to accept many roles I auditioned for, and being asked to accept many roles I ultimately did not accept. But there were and are still times when I am rejected for roles. If it's something I really feel I'm right for and/or would love to do, it hurts. I obsess about it for awhile; I may try to get a word with the director about why he doesn't want me in the role; and then I move on to the next.

How does one obtain representation?

I did a play at the American Academy and it was attended by Juliet Taylor and Marion Dougherty. They are very talented casting directors. They saw me and spoke with the manager, Bill Teusch, about me. He came to see the play, signed on as my manager (he is no longer my manager), and he introduced me to agents.

What do you look for when choosing a project?

I look to see if it would be a role I would enjoy playing. I look at the people involved: director, other actors, production company, etc. I certainly look at whether I like the script, not so much whether it will be liked commercially.

What is the most frustrating and then the most gratifying part of being an actor?

The most frustrating part of being an actor is believing strongly in certain aspects of your character, or of the script, and watching them get dissipated by the committees who tend to make films these days. It is frustrating to have filmmakers think of you as only being capable of doing what they've seen you do before and not giving you a chance to prove the range of your abilities. I found it frustrating to watch an embarrassing number of years go by before television and films began to delve into creating roles for anyone other than white actors in any significant way.

How does one sustain a career in this industry?

The way to sustain a career is closely married to the way you sustain a friendship. You need to have regard for every single person on the set and whom you come into contact with along the way. I feel it's important to "stay plugged-in"—that is to say, it's important to see plays and films that are being made, to keep putting your best energy into all the work you do. Once you start working, don't get hooked up with a manager or agent who has "turndown fever." Saying "no" to too many projects may make your representative feel like a big shot, but it does nothing for you. Work makes work.

At this stage of your career, what are your biggest challenges?

My greatest challenges are to insulate myself as an actor and to still balance other priorities and keep my life functioning smoothly. Being an actor requires certain disciplines in terms of staying in shape, getting enough sleep, eating properly, staying out of chaos—though a certain aspect of the artistic spirit sometimes pulls us in other directions. There are also a lot of superfluous activities that come along with the career—publicity and promoting projects you believe in can be a full-time job on its own, for instance. Answering questions for a book like this is a welcome opportunity, but also a real responsibility.

TOM SKERRITT

An extremely versatile actor, Tom has starred in a wide range of films. His credits include many different roles in such films as M*A*S*H, Alien, Steel Magnolias, Top Gun, *and* A River Runs Through It. *On television, he had a recurring role in* Cheers, *and is currently the star of the popular television series* Picket Fences.

How did you get started in your career?

I did theater in Michigan, quite by accident, with the purpose at the time to overcome shyness and being self-conscious. As I got more involved, I became interested in directing. I then transferred to UCLA to pursue directing, but I felt if I was going to direct, I should know something about acting and writing. So I started that process. I happened to be doing a theater play locally in Los Angeles, and some guys that were doing a low budget feature saw me and asked me to act in it. I thought it was a good way to learn directing. But I did continue to act and here I am all these years later, still learning about film.

Did you attend any acting schools?

No, I just did theater.

How do you prepare yourself for auditions?

I haven't auditioned in many years. I was very fortunate that somebody would see me and make me an offer, so I came in the front door on this one. As I recall, when I had auditions, I would go in with a positive attitude, giving the illusion of not needing the job.

Having done both television and film work, can you explain the differences between them?

Time factor: television is a more condensed version of someone's reality, and features are more theatrical...more of a realistic portrayal in characterization and evolution of plot line.

TOM SKERRITT

In the face of rejection, how do you maintain a sense of security?

I keep a sense of humor! You are constantly putting yourself on the line all the time. You either sink or swim. If you swim, you get stronger and better at your craft, as you do in life.

Is there anything specific you look for when choosing a project?

Ideally, I look for a project that you would pay seven dollars to go see. Secondly, I look for a good character.

What is the most frustrating and then the most gratifying part of being an actor?

The most frustrating is the downtime between jobs. I am usually busy between filmwork, but I think, for actors in general, it is the time not working that is so hard. People need a reason to get up in the morning. This inconsistent film business can make you feel insecure (it's the same for crew members, as well) when you don't know where the next dollar is coming from. That is perhaps the most frustrating aspect of the industry. The most gratifying thing for me, is to be able to contribute to a great film such as *A River Runs Through It*.

How do you sustain your career?

I think you have to have other things to do besides think about when the phone is going to ring. You really have to have a whole other life besides this, whether it's writing or painting—some kind of hobby. You need something compatible and creative. You have to keep the juices flowing!

Do you think it is necessary for actors to live in New York or L.A. when starting their careers?

If you really want to act, I would say that you need to be in New York, because of the theater. However, to really make a living you have to come to Los Angeles.

At this stage of your career, what are your biggest challenges?

I don't see it so much as a challenge. I guess I try to keep getting stronger, better—I try to keep growing. You just can't stop!

What is your advice to someone just starting out?

Go to college. Get a life education and a formal education. If you are going to have any durability in this business, you must be worldly.

JOHN TRAVOLTA

John Travolta made his motion picture debut in the classic horror film Carrie. *That role led him to his starring role in the made-for-television movie* The Boy in the Plastic Bubble. *Eventually he landed the starring role in the hit motion picture* Saturday Night Fever, *which earned him an Academy Award nomination. In 1987, he starred in Harold Pinter's* The Dumbwaiter *(directed by Robert Altman for ABC Television), which won several international awards, including being placed in ABC's Hall of Fame. John's other film credits include the smash hit* Grease, Urban Cowboy, Blow Out, *and* Look Who's Talking. *He recently completed work on Quentin Tarantino's* Pulp Fiction, *which won an award at this year's Cannes Film Festival.*

Did education have a bearing on what you do today?

Since I wasn't formally trained, I would not be an expert in giving my opinion. However, my mother was in acting, and I believe acting classes can be a great help for a person considering a career in acting. I hear Milton Kasalas gives an excellent class.

What advice would you give someone who is considering a career in acting?

Like many other professions, the amount of genuine interest one has for it will dictate your ability to overcome natural obstacles. So you have to love it, and if you do, I believe you can succeed.

Explain how your career began.

I started through local and community theater in the town of Englewood, New Jersey. I did such plays as *Over Here,* with the Andrews Sisters on Broadway, and I was in the road company of the play *Grease.* I also did *Bye Bye Birdie* at a dinner theater called Club Bene in Morgan, New Jersey, and there I was discovered by my soon-to-be manager, Bob Lemond, who guided my career. I eventually landed the role of "Vinnie Barbarino" on the television show *Welcome Back, Kotter,* which led to my first major film role in *Saturday Night Fever.*

JOHN TRAVOLTA

In the face of rejection, how do you maintain a sense of security?

The way I maintain a sense of security is by applying the teachings of *Dianetics* and Scientology. For me, it has been extremely helpful.

Do you have a philosophy that prepares you for auditions?

The more rehearsal, the better the audition. So practice, I would say, is essential.

What do you look for when choosing a project?

I look for a good story and character appeal for the audience. Getting a good reaction from your audience is very important for me as an actor.

Express the importance of living in a city like L.A. or New York.

New York was pivotal for one simple reason: it was truly accessible in regards to the theater opportunities; that is, trade papers like *Variety, Show Business,* and *Backstage* offered daily opportunities to anyone willing to audition or interview to get a job in the theater.

What advice would you give to someone who has to work a full-time job while pursuing acting?

Get involved in a production that rehearses and performs at night, so that agents and producers have access to your talent.

How does one get an agent?

Make sure that you are seen in productions or theater groups that agents go to. If they don't, invite them. They're often looking for new talent. I also recommend a book, *Everything You Always Wanted To Know About L.A.'s & N.Y.'s Casting Directors...But Were Afraid To Ask,* written by Wendy Shawn.

At this stage of your career, what are your greatest challenges?

Continuing to make it work. It's a full-time job.

VANNA WHITE

For millions of TV viewers all over the world, Vanna White is a household name. She rose to fame as the cohost of TV's most popular game show, Wheel of Fortune. *Today, she enjoys keeping her job on* Wheel of Fortune *fresh and alive for all her faithful viewers. Vanna resides in Los Angeles with her husband and newborn baby boy.*

Would you briefly explain how you got started in your career?

Ever since I was ten years old, when I saw my uncle (Christopher George) on television, I wanted to be a movie star. That was the only thing I wanted to do. After graduating from high school, I moved to Atlanta, Georgia and started modeling professionally and taking acting classes. In 1980 I moved to Los Angeles hoping to become a big star, and very quickly my dreams were shattered by all the rejection I got. Like everyone else, you think you can come to Los Angeles and become a star overnight, but it doesn't happen that way. So I did small jobs here and there, like waitressing. In November, 1982, after auditioning with two hundred other women, I got *Wheel of Fortune*. It's been wonderful ever since! That was my first big break, and ten years later I still count my blessings and appreciate my job.

How do you maintain a sense of security in the face of rejection?

It is very difficult. You feel ugly, unwanted...every negative feeling you can imagine hits you when you are rejected. I would say that I got one out of a hundred interviews I went on. That's a lot of rejection.

Specifically, is there anything you do to not feel insecure?

What I did, and the way I handled it, which was interesting, was that I gained twenty-five pounds! So I must have gone to food for all that rejection. I guess I made up for it by eating.

◆

VANNA WHITE

Are there any acting classes in Los Angeles that you can recommend?

I studied with Vincent Chase in the beginning and then with Rick Walters. My most recent acting coach was Roy London.

How do you prepare yourself for auditions?

If it's a commercial audition or a movie audition, obviously you have to read and become familiar with the script. You practice with it in front of a mirror, or privately with your coach. Have your friends help you. Just become familiar with the material—learn it inside and out.

What advice would you give someone who has to work full-time in another profession while pursuing acting at the same time?

If acting is what you want to do, don't give up on your dream. We all have to support ourselves one way or another, and you can't give up your job to pursue an acting career because you never know from day to day. Even the biggest star doesn't have a job after the last day of his movie. So you always have to be aware.

Would you recommend theater groups where aspiring actors can go to gain performance experience?

Absolutely! I would recommend trying to stay involved with whatever it is you are doing, including attending acting classes. Learn as much as you can, stay current, be familiar, and practice! By all means, participate in theater groups and do whatever you can.

What suggestions can you give with regard to obtaining representation?

People say, "Oh, well I'm the biggest agency in town." That doesn't mean anything to me. My suggestion when looking for an agent is to find someone that believes in you. They don't have to be the biggest agent, they just have to believe in you and you have to believe in them.

What do you find is the most frustrating and then the most gratifying part of being an actress?

The most frustrating part is the rejection and not getting the part...feeling that negative side. No matter what, it hurts when you don't get the job. You take it personally. The gratifying side of acting, for me, is the people who come to me for autographs...the letters I receive...maybe I can put a smile on someone's face or give them a suggestion to a problem...maybe I can help them in some way.

Can you give any advice on how to sustain your career?

My suggestion is to treat everyone equally. Sometimes when people become successful, they forget those people who helped them up the ladder. I think when you do forget those people, you are bound to come down a lot harder.

At this stage of your career, what are your greatest challenges?

My greatest challenges are just maintaining what I have. Who knows where *Wheel of Fortune* is going to be tomorrow? I'm always aware of this ending. I try to keep it fresh and alive and keep people interested.

Have you considered getting into film?

I have considered getting into film. But right now I am very happy where I am, and it would mean a lot of traveling and being on the road, away from my husband. If something comes along, that's okay, but I'm not pursuing it.

DAPHNE ZUNIGA

Fans of the hit television show Melrose Place *will recognize Daphne as "Jo," the streetwise fashion photographer. Her other television credits include* Quarterback Princess *and* Stone Pillow, *with Lucille Ball. Daphne made her film debut in* The Sure Thing, *and has appeared in films such as* Gross Anatomy, Spaceballs, Vision Quest, The Fly II, Staying Together, *and* The Last Rites.

How did your career begin?

The first play I did was when I was twelve years old. Before that, I did plays in my neighborhood. I always loved pretending and loved having an audience. I continued acting in school and community plays. I then went on to college at the University of Southern California where I majored in theater. It wasn't a real intellectual decision as an adult—it was something I wanted to do because I loved acting. In my junior year, my roommate asked me to do a scene with her for an agent. They signed us both the next day. That was in 1983.

I didn't expect this to happen. I expected to be unemployed for the next ten years, living in New York. Literally, I thought this is what one had to do. I think there were more agents looking at actors doing scenes back then. It's very different now. I was very lucky.

What advice would you give someone just starting out?

My advice would be to act, wherever and however possible. If you are in school, participate in plays and see if you really like acting. It's tempting for people, especially [those] coming to Hollywood. They want the results of being famous or successful, and it doesn't happen that easily for most people. It's very trying and very difficult and challenging on every level, physical and emotional. You really have to love doing it. It's always good to find a teacher or a director who will guide you so that you can see if you love it so much, you'll find out there is no other alternative.

Is it important to live in a city like New York or Los Angeles when starting out?

I attended high school in Vermont, and when I graduated I did summer stock in a really small company in a very small state. After that, I wanted to come to New York or Los Angeles. I did

DAPHNE ZUNIGA

not want to be a big fish in a small pond, but rather a tiny little polliwog in a huge ocean. I wanted to be where the biggest challenges were.

I have also read stories about people that came up in regional theater, such as Kevin Kline and Meryl Streep. They have done theater forever, so when their film came they already had an immense background. I don't have that type of background because I came to Los Angeles right away. I don't think it's an either or [situation]. There are no steps to follow or rewards following these steps. That's why people become disappointed and end up in bad situations. You really need to know that this is the only thing you want to do and go for it. If you decide to come to Los Angeles, you must make sure that you can have chances to act in class or in showcases. If not, go where you can get the most training.

Can you recommend any good acting classes?

I am really bad at this. However, I trained with Peggy Fuery and her husband, who have since passed away. During their heyday, this was great training. I also studied with John Lehne in Burbank, California. I don't want to give away my personal trainer because his classes are too full!

How did you maintain a sense of security when faced with rejection?

I've done a lot of hitting pillows, crying, and screaming in the car. We all feel rejection. It's something you can't deny. When I was in college, a woman came to speak to us. She was performing in *The Fantastiks* on Broadway. She told us she had two hundred and sixty-five rejections before she got this part. I told myself, "I've had five—so I have two hundred and sixty to go." You have to know, through it all, that this is how it's going to be. And this is the challenge, because on every level you are going to have rejection. I am on *Melrose Place* right now, but I had ten years of auditioning and did different things during that time. I did ten movies to one hundred auditions. Every rejection will be painful—some not as painful as others—but you just need to go on. That is why you really need to love this profession.

Explain the difference between acting in films and acting on television.

Television goes much faster. You have to cover a lot of material in each day. In many ways it's more tiring, but since you don't get chances to rehearse, it gives you a chance to be more spontaneous. It's hard not to rehearse, because that is what I love to do. In film you get more rehearsal time, but there is more waiting around for hours on the set—not so in television.

What do you look for when choosing a project?

The character is very important. On *Melrose Place*, I got a chance to develop the character with the producer and writers. The great thing in television is that your character gets to change and grow. In the past, I would choose projects because of who was directing or because of the actors involved. The story is also an extremely important part of choosing a project.

How do you prepare for an audition?

If I can get the material, I try to get it as far ahead of time as possible. I go over the material and learn the lines, jot down any ideas and anything that comes to mind about the character, whether it be physical or emotional, or just things that come to mind. I try not to just get into learning the lines. I had a teacher who said that you have to be like a detective: ask as many questions as possible about anything in the text. I also use something that stimulates me to inspire the audition, such as music.

The biggest thing is to deal with the fear you're going to have. God knows how many times I've gone in and my fear has shut me down. Try to relax and know that these people want to like you—they are not the enemy. When you come in the room, they've seen so many people and they would love for you to blow them away. You have to realize that they are on your side, so try not to be afraid. This is your chance to act. Enjoy that moment because it could be a fun experience.

What is the most frustrating and then the most gratifying part of being an actress?

What's really frustrating is the time between jobs. Sitting and waiting to be asked to do what you love to do is very frustrating. I once went a year and a half without working, and frustrating was a mild word. There are frustrations on the set, lack of rehearsal time, certain obstacles you have to face. Gratifying are those times when you are working and you have done a great deal of work on a part and something special happens during your actual performance. It doesn't happen all the time, but when it happens, it is so gratifying. A successful show is gratifying, and hearing people tell me they like the show or the work I've done is extremely gratifying.

What suggestions can you give regarding representation?

It's a real evil, catch-22 situation. That's the one thing I feel so lucky about: that I did not have to look for an agent. My suggestion would be to start by sending out photos and doing showcases where agents can come see you perform. Also, having film work on yourself is always helpful.

At this stage of your career, what are your biggest challenges?

To grow as a person and to continue to reveal other sides of myself with my work. To push myself beyond the safety of what I already know I can do.

SCREENWRITERS

BOB GALE

*Originally an engineering student at Tulane University, this suburban St. Louis native soon
realized he wanted to follow a more creative path. He enrolled at USC Cinema School where he
met Robert Zemeckis. The two became a team and eventually produced screenplays for* 1941,
I Wanna Hold Your Hand, Used Cars *and* Back To The Future, *which earned them an
Academy Award nomination for best original screenplay. Bob wrote the screenplays for* Back To
The Future, Part II *and* Part III, *wrote and directed an episode of* Tales From The Crypt,
and is currently working on an interactive film project for Sony Pictures Entertainment.

How did your career begin?

I always enjoyed creative writing, even in grade school. And I started making movies as a hobby
in high school. I went to engineering school at Tulane, but after one semester, I decided it wasn't
for me. A guy in my dorm, who knew my hobby was filmmaking, told me there were film
schools in California. So I applied and got into USC.

In my junior year, 1971, I met Bob Zemeckis. We both had similar tastes in films and both
wanted to make Hollywood movies, so we started collaborating on a low-budget horror script
even before we finished school. After graduation, Zemeckis started hanging around Universal
Studios, trying to figure out how to get a directing job. He heard that the TV series *McCloud*
was short one script, so he and I banged one out in ten days. Universal optioned it. We found
out about two other series that needed scripts, and made two more sales.

This was in 1974, when networks would order a full twenty-two episode season of just about
everything; these were shows in the bottom of the ratings which A-list writers didn't want to work
on. With our third sale, Universal offered us a seven-year contract to write television. We turned
it down because television didn't give us enough credibility to get an agent, who had advised us
that if we wanted to write features, we should sit down and write a feature script. So we did. We
used our USC connections to get alumnus John Milius to read it—and he liked it. Milius had

BOB GALE

just made *The Wind and the Lion* at MGM and had been given a four-picture deal. He decided to hire us to write a script for him, which became the movie *1941*. That was the first feature we got paid real money to write, and Milius deserves the credit for giving us our first big break.

Is film school important today?

You don't have to go to film school, but it certainly doesn't hurt, and probably helps. It's been over twenty years since I went to school, so undoubtedly a lot of things are different now. However, what I enjoyed was being surrounded by people who were as fanatical about movies as I was. School creates a structured environment where you are required to produce films, or scripts, or whatever, and thus you have a clear motivation and deadline to do the work.

In a creative field, having a reason to get off your butt and be creative is important. And when you're paying the kind of money that film school costs, you're motivated to want to get your money's worth.

Is it important to write every day?

I don't physically write every day because sometimes I have nothing to write. However, I'm usually thinking about a script even if I'm not actually pounding the keys on my computer. I believe that you shouldn't take a trip until you know where you are going. Some people force themselves to write everyday, which does create a discipline, and motivation and discipline are essential habits to cultivate in order to be a writer. I happen to be a good self-starter. If you're not, forcing yourself to write every day is a good idea. A writing partner can also help. When you're in the same room with somebody else, you eventually start writing because you'll feel guilty about wasting the other person's time by just goofing off.

Where do you get your ideas?

I don't know. They just happen—sometimes totally out of the blue, or because of something that I see on the news, in a book, something someone says. There's no science to it. Ray Bradbury once said that the process of getting an idea is like trying to behead the Medusa: if you face her directly, you're turned to stone; but if you creep up on her sideways, you just might nail her. That's a good analogy.

How do your characters evolve from your basic concept?

Usually, the concept dictates who the characters are going to have to be. In *Back To The Future* we had a kid who was going to travel through time. We decided he should travel via a time machine.

We had to figure out where this time machine would come from. Obviously, somebody had to build it. And so we created Doc Brown, making him into a wild-eyed, crazed inventor—the type of guy who could build a time machine in his garage. When you see Doc Brown the first time, you just know his invention is going to work!

And then a relationship had to be created so that Marty would know Doc Brown. The story wouldn't have worked if the time machine had been built by the Government—and the time machine probably wouldn't have worked either! This goes back to what I was saying about first needing a destination in order to plan your trip. We needed a time machine, and Doc Brown was how we got there.

Do you ever let anyone read a work-in-progress?

Very rarely. I'd much rather have a draft from beginning to end that I've done over myself. Sometimes I'll get halfway through a script and come up with a new idea that should be planted in the first ten pages to make the back half of the script work properly. I don't like to give pages to anyone and then have to make excuses about them. And the fact is, a huge part of writing is rewriting.

Do you ever have a specific actor in mind when writing a character?

Sometimes I'll imagine someone with a very distinctive style of talking, like a James Cagney or a John Wayne, just to help me create a certain rhythm to the dialog and make sure that each character has a unique speech pattern. Obviously, the *Back To The Future* sequels were written with specific actors in mind. And in *Used Cars* we created the character of Jim the Mechanic for Frank McRae, who we knew pretty well.

Have you ever thought about directing?

Yes. I directed an episode of *Tales From The Crypt,* and now I want to direct a feature…from one of my own screenplays. That's my primary challenge right now.

What skills should a writer have?

Going beyond the obvious, such as literacy, you need to be thick-skinned and be able to handle rejection, because a writer's life is full of rejection. *Back To The Future* was written in 1980–81, but took four years to get made. It was turned down by everyone. The first draft of *Trespass* was written in 1977, fourteen years before it was made. You have to have perseverance.

BOB GALE

When faced with rejection, how did you maintain a sense of security?

Let's put that in the present tense: my work still gets rejected. The advantage of being a known writer is I get rejected faster! In other words, they will read my script before one written by an unknown writer, but they still say "no" more often than "yes." I try not to take it personally, but I still get depressed. Then I have to remind myself that it's happened before, and I'm not the first person this has ever happened to, nor will I be the last.

How does one get an agent?

Somehow. But it's important to realize that just because you have an agent doesn't mean he'll be able to get you a job or sell your script. Usually, the amount of attention you get from an agent is a function of how much money you're bringing in. When Bob and I started off, we did our own hustling. Once you find someone who wants to buy your work, it's not too hard to get an agent, since you've already done the hardest part, which is finding someone who wants to pay you money.

What are the most frustrating and gratifying parts of being a writer?

In terms of the actual writing process, the most frustrating thing is the discipline. When the script is finished, it's the rejection. The most gratifying part is sitting in a theater with an audience and having them respond to the material the way I intended—laughing, or being scared, or cheering—that's a real high.

Any further advice?

If you're a writer, then write. Write the script. Don't say "I have an idea for a script." Write it! The great thing about approaching the industry through writing is that, assuming you can write a script in the correct form, and that it's fairly literate, your finished screenplay will look as professional as mine. A producer or studio executive can respond to it as finished work, ready to go. I don't recommend writing outlines or treatments (except for yourself). It's better to write the script.

And be aware of what's makeable, and what isn't. Use some common sense about audience taste. And above all, be passionate about what you're writing about. If you care about it, chances are, it'll be better.

LARRY HERTZOG

Larry has written many episodes for television, as well as pilots and movies of the week. His credits include episodes of Hart to Hart, Walker: Texas Ranger, Raven, Down Delaware Road, *a pilot for ABC entitled* Tin Man, *and a pilot for CBS entitled* Bodyguard. *He also created the show* Starbuck *with Stephen J. Cannell.*

Did your education have any bearing on what you do today?

Yes. Getting out of the educational system as soon as I could gave me the opportunity to get started sooner and have fewer silly ideas about things.

Did you have any formal training?

No, and to be honest, most of my peers—other writer/producers that I've worked with—did not either. I don't really believe that anything creative can be taught. In the real world, though, it can be learned.

In addition to good writing skills, what other tools would one need?

Believe it or not, writers need a lot of the same skills actors do—particularly in terms of a tough hide. You are going to be rejected all the time. You are going to hear a million different opinions. I think that a lot of people who dream about being writers don't really imagine how tough it is in this way. I think that they have some notion of a quiet attic grotto, a glass of Chablis—a studious tomb where we listen to the Muses speak. They've clearly never been in a development meeting. We constantly hear that there are countless people out there banging on the door, trying to get in, but only a few make it. What's left out of that statement is that not all these people have the same qualifications. It's not a level playing field in which some get lucky and some don't.

I really believe that luck has little to do with it. Or, at least you make your luck. So in terms of tools, I guess a tough hide and a damn-the-torpedoes, full-speed-ahead kind of attitude. I mean, everyone wants to be rich and thin—but wanting isn't enough.

LARRY HERTZOG

What suggestions would you give someone trying to obtain representation?

There is no one way to do it. There are no rules. You have to have the attitude that "I'm coming. The doors are locked and welded shut in front of me." Again, it's that "do it or die" proposition. In terms of getting an agent, it's the same way. The first thing you should do is write, write, and write! Get your material out there. Through that process, you might pick up an agent.

Of course you can always try the traditional route: call the Writers Guild and get a list of accredited agents. When I got my first agent, one of the things she said impressed her about me was that I did not have a script under my arm—I had three. While she was reading them, I was working on my fourth! That's what I came out here to do. I think this agent not only liked the material she was reading, but saw someone who came here to write come hell or high water.

When you are writing a script, do you ever share it before it's completed?

Sure. I have my "test group"—mostly people I trust, or writers that I respect. Ultimately, though, when the day is over, the only judgement that's worth anything is your own. If you write to please someone else, you are probably going to fail.

In the face of rejection, how do you maintain your security?

A piece of old baby blanket and a pacifier. I don't really know. I don't have an answer. I think that one of the hardest things is that you get beat up all the time and are expected to come back fresh. By the way, how much you get beat up has nothing to do with your status as a writer. You can be making seven figures and you will be equally hammered on. It's a very egalitarian system. You should pick up any one of William Goldman's books to confirm that "they" don't play favorites.

What is the most frustrating and most gratifying parts of being a writer?

Gratifying? What's that? We're in a business where creative people are trying to sell to administrators and business people. It's very frustrating [trying] to get them to see what you see...to understand how specific thoughts and ideas are going to come together and make a final project. Of course, beyond all the nightmares of selling, there is the pure joy of doing it! What can I say? It's a real kick to be out there shooting film, putting it together. There are times when it's hard to believe that you're getting paid to do this kind of thing.

At this stage of your career, what are your greatest challenges?

Maintaining my sanity and being able to continue to write without too much angst or lower back pain.

DAVID KOEPP

David Koepp grew up in Wisconsin and graduated from UCLA's film school in 1986. His first film was the thriller Apartment Zero, *which he cowrote and produced with director Martin Donovan in 1988. His other writing credits include* Bad Influence, Death Becomes Her, Jurassic Park, Carlito's Way, The Paper, *and* The Shadow.

Can you explain how you got started in your career?

I was in Madison, Wisconsin, at college, acting and writing. I had a professor who was directing me in a play and also taught a playwriting class. He asked me, "So, what do you want to do?" And I said, "Either act or write movies." He said, "Well, after directing you as an actor and watching you write, I suggest you write." So I went west and applied to the UCLA Film School and finished my undergrad there. Film school was primarily valuable for the friends that I made. We were all aspiring writers and started to read each other's material and exchange comments, which many of us do still—and it's really helpful. I think a community of writers is essential, much more productive than the film school itself.

Do you feel that going to film school is essential for someone who wants to write?

No, absolutely not. I think I learned a lot more after I left school. After I left, I had a day job at this company that bought U.S. titles for foreign distributors (mostly video). It was a job where I had to read a lot of scripts and see a lot of movies, and no matter how good or bad they were, it was helpful to sort of immerse myself in what I wanted to do. The only way you can get good at writing is by doing it—a lot. It takes, for me anyway, half-a-dozen scripts to even become competent. And inspired is even further down the road. While a lot of people write screenplays, I think so many of them are unsuccessful at it because they just don't give it long enough. It takes a long time.

DAVID KOEPP

Where do you derive your ideas from?

That's always the hardest question to answer because I don't know. I did a movie called *Bad Influence* that hit me at the corner of Pico and Sepulveda, and I wrote a first draft in six weeks. Sometimes it all kind of drops out of the sky on you—a whole movie—and other times you get a little bit at a time. Martin Donovan, a guy I've done a couple of movies with, and I did this movie, *Death Becomes Her,* but that one was bit by bit. We started it in '87, when one of us had this much of an idea. And then six months later, another added a bit more, and so on, for several years. Some ideas come piecemeal; others just drop all at once. And you never know.

For **Bad Influence,** *you said that you got the idea on the corner of Pico and Sepulveda. Do any ideas ever come to you from something that happened in your life? Are there any similarities?*

Yes. Actually, that one was somewhat-based on true experience. My old boss liked to surf, and he knew this guy from the beach, kind of a free spirit, kind of a wild guy. One time when we were out of town at some convention, we came back and he'd ripped off my boss's house and stolen his money. I got to thinking, once you let somebody into your life, what if it turns out you made a mistake? How do you get them out? This is hardly an original idea now—there have been a zillion movies about it in the last few years. But back in '88 or '87, it seemed a little fresher.

When you get an idea or start to write a screenplay, do you ever have someone in mind to play the part?

I consciously try not to, but it's unavoidable because I think when the actor is cast, you're going to have to write for them anyway. So if you start doing it now, you're fencing yourself in. Really, writing the first draft of the script is the one time you get to make all the calls. So I try not to think of somebody, because then it becomes that actor and not my character.

The first screenplay that you wrote, was it something that was recognized?

No. The first several I wrote weren't very good at all. The first one I wrote was in college with a friend of mine in Madison. It was based on a play he'd written. And it was a great idea, but we didn't write a very good script. Eight or nine years after we first wrote this script, one of us said, "Hey, I know what our problem always was with that." So, he's writing it again with this new idea. That's how they go. You try and try and try and you never quite know what your problems are...and then all of the sudden it hits you.

Can you describe the development of your writing now as compared to the beginning?

I think I'm a lot better than I was, because like any discipline, the more you practice the better you get. In screenwriting, the more times you've been in impossible situations and gotten out of them, the more tricks you have up your sleeve. Hopefully I don't make the same mistakes. I know what I don't do as well and I try harder with that.

In the face of rejection, how do you maintain a sense of security?

It's hard, but I don't think it's as hard as acting, because in acting the rejection is personalized. They say, "You are not right. You're wrong for the part." In screenwriting they say, "We don't like your script." Which seems like it ought to hurt less, but it never does. It never gets any easier. Every time I give somebody a script, I go through this seven-to-ten-day honeymoon period where I think it's perfect and I think they're all naturally going to agree with me. And of course they don't, because it's not, and it crushes me every single time. So, "No, it never gets any easier."

Do you think it's important then to share your script with other people?

Vital (for me, anyway). Part of the writing process is those two or three friends whose opinions you really respect, who have absolutely no interest in the project, giving me their honest opinions. I couldn't write without it.

Besides understanding structure and being a creative person, what other skills would a person need to be a good writer?

Discipline is a huge one, because you just don't get any better unless you do it a lot. And you have to be tireless. You have to be willing to go in and rip everything apart and start over. You can't be thin-skinned. You've got to be able to take criticism, even when you know they're wrong. You just have to let that wash over you and keep listening, because you never know from whom or when will come a very good point.

What do you find is the most frustrating and then the most gratifying part of being a screen-writer?

The most frustrating is that I seem to make the same mistakes all the time. Also, the classic thing that writers get no respect: there's always somebody else taking credit for the best lines. I find that very frustrating. Gratifying is when you see it and you really like it. There's no feeling like it. And

DAVID KOEPP

when you see wonderful actors, or an actress like Meryl Streep, doing such a wonderful job with the material and bringing the people that you've known for years to life, it's the strangest, most wonderful feeling in the world.

What helpful suggestions can you give someone with regard to obtaining representation?

Don't worry about it. That's the best advice I can give. By far, the hardest part about becoming a screenwriter and getting paid for it is writing a good screenplay. I had a screenwriting professor in college who said, "If you write a good screenplay, you can leave it in the middle of the [Highway] 405 and somebody will find it and make a movie out of it." Which is really true. Once the script is done, compared to the arduous task of writing that script, finding an agent will be a piece of cake. William Goldman gives great advice. He says, "Call everybody you know." See if they have any connection at all in Hollywood and call them up.

At this stage of your career, what are the biggest challenges?

I think any writer who says he doesn't eventually want to try directing is probably lying. I'd like to try it and see. I've been really lucky to work with the people I've worked with. But there is this gnawing sensation of, "I wonder what it would have looked like if it had been my vision all the way."

What further advice can you give to a person wanting to pursue a career as a screenwriter?

Screenwrite. If you want to be a screenwriter, screenwrite. Take some classes. UCLA Extension's pretty good. There's a lot of courses out there. You don't have to go to film school. Take a class where you meet other people and commiserate with other people who are trying to write, and you will pick up a few things. Read—you know, the "bibles." *The Art of Dramatic Writing* is very important; so is Syd Field's *Screenplay.* But mostly just do it. Face the ugly, daily job of putting words on blank paper.

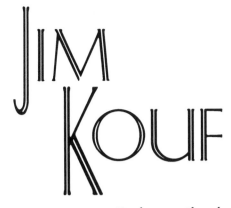

JIM KOUF

Jim has contributed to the writing and development of such films as Aladdin *and* White Fang. *His first feature, cowritten with David Greenwalt, was* Class. *The pair went on to write* American Dreamer, Secret Admirer, *and* Up the Creek. *In 1986, he made his directorial debut with* Miracles, *and then went on to direct* Disorganized Crime *(which he also wrote). His other writing credits include* Stakeout *and* The Hidden. *Jim has since teamed with Lynn Bigelow (shown here with Jim in the picture at left) to form Kouf / Bigelow Productions.*

Would you briefly explain how you started your writing career?

I started out making films in high school, not because I wanted to be in the film business, but rather because films were easier to make than term papers were to write. I basically hated writing, and I avoided it whenever possible. Then I went to college and wound up majoring in English and minoring in History. The English degree had several required writing courses, and still, I remember not finding much enjoyment in writing—not until I had my first dramatic writing course. That was the first time I actually liked writing. And it was the first course I did very well in.

So, I figured I must have some kind of knack for it. And I decided I would be a playwright. Playwrights, I soon discovered upon moving back to Los Angeles, lived in New York, and I didn't have the money to move to New York. But I did know a sound man, Buzz Knudson, who worked at Todd-AO. I asked Buzz for help, and he introduced me to Callie Curtis, who made industrial films. She and her husband had been television writers for several years before she turned her attention to industrials. I sat down with Callie and told her I wanted to write films, and she told me if I wanted to be a writer, I had better write. She gave me a television script to read and learn the format from and told me to pick out a series I liked and write an episode for it.

Then she sent me away. I picked *M*A*S*H*. I didn't realize I was starting at the top, but it was the show I most admired for its writing. So I wrote one script and gave it to Callie and she said, "Okay, you can write. Now write another." So I wrote a second and then a third. She then tried to help me get an agent to represent the scripts. She got the agent and I had very high hopes, but he couldn't sell the scripts. And I was back to square one, almost, except I had attracted the attention of an agent. And that was a start.

What was the first recognized script you wrote?

The first script that received a lot of attention was *American Dreamer*. I wrote it with another writer, David Greenwalt, who was my writing partner for several scripts. *American Dreamer* was a rewrite of a script owned by Mel Simon. And it made the rounds and made our agent's job a little easier getting us meetings. That's how we wound up with Marty Ransohoff, whom we wrote *Class* for. *Class* was the first time we ever sold a story on a pitch.

How do your characters evolve from your basic concept?

I'm not sure which comes first—the concept or the character. Stories seem to start in several different ways: I find a character I like, or a setting or an incident (it's one ingredient at a time), throw them into a pot, stir them around and hope it comes out edible. But usually I start with a character.

Probably the easiest example is *Stakeout*. I wanted to tell a simple story about two guys stuck in a room. I wanted to do this because I wanted them to be forced to talk with one another—to reveal themselves in a limited space. I don't know why this intrigued me, except that it's a basic set-up: two guys in a room—what do they talk about? I then searched for the reason why they were stuck in the room. The searching ended with a stakeout. Okay, I had a reason for the guys to be stuck, and they had to be cops. So the next step was: who were they staking out? When I hit on a woman, and then on one of them for the woman, the rest of the idea fell into place quickly.

Is it important to write everyday?

If one wants to make a living at writing, it's very important. I try to write five pages a day, whether I feel like it or not, and whether the pages are good or bad. It seems to me that writing is like mining: the more dirt you move, the more gold you find. And sometimes you have to move a lot of dirt to find anything at all.

While you are working on a script, do you let others review your work before it's complete?

I usually don't let anyone read a script until a draft is complete. Then I let my partner, Lynn Bigelow, read it first. If she likes it and laughs in the right places, then I take it back and make another pass through it. A lot of my story work goes into the outlines. Then I write a treatment. Then I take on the script. The more details I can add before I attempt the script usually means fewer mistakes during the screenplay.

Do you ever write a script with a specific actor or actress in mind?

Not usually, unless it's specifically requested by the studio. Usually, I try to create the best character possible within the context of the story. Very seldom do I describe physical characteristics at length, unless it's important to the story. But a screenwriter has to face a certain reality of moviemaking: the studios, for the most part, want a star...and there are very few stars.

What is the most frustrating and then the most gratifying part of being a screenwriter?

Let me reverse the order of your question. The most gratifying part of being a screenwriter is finishing a script and turning it in to the studio and having everyone get excited about it and calling you and saying how wonderful it is and how great you are. Life, then, is worth living. Everything after that (story notes, director's notes, actor's notes, studio changes, director changes, actor changes, one-sheets, release dates, critics' personal potshots, the weather, traffic) is frustrating, to one degree or another. The first draft is the best. It's the only time you're going steady.

What is your opinion on film schools?

That's difficult to answer, since I didn't go to film school. But I don't think it's necessary if writing is what interests you. I think a background in literature is more important—including theater. For a screenwriter, the ability to tell a story, however you learn that, whether in school or sittin' on your granpappy's knee, is the only thing that matters.

Can you recommend any books that would help with script structure?

I never used any "how-to" books. My recommendation is to read good writing. Read Steinbeck and Mark Twain, and then read Goldman's *Butch Cassidy and the Sundance Kid* and Newman and Benton's *Bonnie and Clyde*. Read the best around and then try to be better. Chances are you won't, but you might as well shoot high. But pushed to recommend books on writing, I'd suggest Lajos Egri's *The Art of Dramatic Writing* or Michael Hauge's *Writing Screenplays That Sell*.

JIM KOUF

What other skills does a screenwriter need?

Experience—as much as possible, in as many areas as possible. To be a good writer, in general, you have to be an interested person. You have to want to know what makes people tick. You cannot limit your life to Hollywood, or to any one thing. You should explore. When you're not writing, get out of the house. Go someplace. Do something...and I don't mean go to the movies.

What suggestions do you have for obtaining representation?

If you write a good script, you will get an agent—it's that simple. But let someone else tell you it's a good script. I get tired of writers telling me how good their screenplay is, only to find out how wrong they were. And if the script is good, the word will get around rather quickly. Hollywood loves discovering new writing talent—we're still the least expensive part of the process. But register the script with The Writers Guild first. The Guild can also provide a list of agents who will accept unsolicited manuscripts.

At this stage of your career, what are your biggest challenges?

Writing a good script. It never gets easier, but it does get more difficult. The more screenplays you write, the less paths untried. And there is always the mystery of, "If I write a script that has been well-received and everything seems to work on the page, why does this movie stink?"

What further advice would you give an aspiring writer?

Only if you love writing should you get involved with Hollywood. Don't write for the money or the fame. Write because you love movies and want to make a great one. It's a great business if you're good at it. If you're not, it ain't much fun.

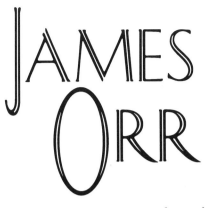

JAMES ORR

A native of Canada, the multi-talented James Orr (Director/Producer/Screenwriter) attended film school at York University in Toronto before being selected for a directing fellowship at the prestigious American Film Institute in Los Angeles. James and his partner Jim Cruickshank are one of the most successful and respected writer-producer teams in Hollywood. Their writing credits include the smash hits Three Men and A Baby, Sister Act 2, *and* Mr. Destiny, *which James also directed. He and his partner produced the film* Father of the Bride, *and the television projects* Adventures, Inc., 14 Going On 30, *and the Emmy-nominated* Young Harry Houdini.

How did your career begin?

I essentially started as a film student at a university film school. I went from there to a graduate program at the American Film Institute. One of the things AFI did for me was to get me to Los Angeles, which is a critical part of the equation as far as I'm concerned, in terms of making it in the business. When I finished AFI, I was nowhere, as a lot of film students are upon finishing school. I trained as a director all through my schooling, but you just don't walk out of school and get a directing job. It became very apparent to me, and I think for a lot of others, that the best way to direct movies is to write them.

All the doors in Hollywood are hard to open, but the easiest of the hard doors to open is writing. You can write a spec script on your own, and it's not expensive to do it. Or you can come in with a good idea for a script or a script in its entirety. What you want is for it to be sold, because once it's sold you can get an agent, which usually doesn't happen until you have sold something. Then you have something to build a career on—the first brick of the foundation is laid. I've said this to many people over the years: the best way, the easiest way—and not that it's ever easy—but the easiest of the hard ways is to write.

Is attending film school essential?

No, I don't think so. I think film school has one major benefit. In retrospect it was a big benefit for me. In film school, you can make a lot of errors with impunity. You can play and expand and experiment with impunity. You can't make those kind of errors or experiments in the real world, because very often you don't get more than one or two chances to show that you have some promise. In film school, they are much more forgiving than they are in the real world. If you want to flex your muscles and pay your dues, if you want to play around with the medium and find out what it's about, film school is a great forum in which to do that.

From where do you derive your ideas?

My partner Jim Cruickshank and I tend to consistently do the same category of movies. For lack of a better term, I call it "human comedy," which is comedy with some basic reality—with some emotional truth behind the laughs. Those inspirations come from everyday life; they come from your idle thoughts; they come from a news story—something you saw when you were ten and it moved you. You'll take that and reinvent it in another context.

Is it important to write everyday?

Yes. It's like working out in a gym. If you don't keep working out and you're trying to build your body up, and if you let go for even a week or more, it takes a long time to get it back again. Writing is similar. You have to be always flexing the creative muscle, so when you're put on the spot to deliver, you are better able to deliver. As a writer, you have to prepare all those early years, and I mean *years,* preparing for that one moment. So when opportunity knocks, you can act quickly, be effective, and impress the people you need to impress. And it happens quickly. If you're not prepared, you'll be sitting in the dust.

Besides good writing, what other skills would one need?

I've found that writers tend to be, not always—there are exceptions—very verbal. Being able to communicate verbally is not far off from being able to communicate on the page. There are plenty of exceptions where people don't speak at all and are great writers. But I still think if you can communicate verbally, there's probably a good chance that if you have the discipline, you'll be able to translate that onto the page.

The obvious things one would need are to be observant of the things around you and observant of your emotions. It's also important to be a lifelong student of the audience, to pay attention to what audiences respond to. And that changes year to year. Also, persistency: it took me five years—five miserable years—before I had any glimmer that I made the right decision.

What suggestions can you give with regard to obtaining representation?

The best way to get an agent is to have a sale. Not only are you bringing a piece of material, but you're bringing the fact that you are already saleable. If you don't bring a sale to an agent, but rather a piece of material, they have to make the leap of faith that you are saleable without any proof yet. If you come in with a lot of big ideas, that's a very big leap of faith to make. I'm not saying you won't make it that way, but it's pretty unlikely. Show business is like a casino. You go into show business and it can be very impersonal like a casino. There are a lot of games in the room. You need to be able to pick the game where the odds are most in your favor. You might still lose, but at least you've stacked the odds in your favor.

So in Hollywood, people in the beginning need to take a good look at the business. One thing that helped me a lot early on was [that] I tried to learn how the "Hollywood Machine" worked: the studio system, the network system, how movies are made and distributed, reading the trades—although in the beginning I could not afford the trades, so I would go to the library to read them.

How did you maintain a sense of security when faced with rejection?

I go back to the casino metaphor: you can't go up to a game and bet everything you have because if you lose, you'll be devastated. So, you have to be a smart player and play a little bit here and there, so if you lose, you're not destroyed.

What is the most frustrating and then the most gratifying part of being a writer?

A lot of writers would not say this, but my partner and I really enjoy the writing process. We have been writing together for sixteen years, and we know each other very well and make each other laugh. So the actual process is very gratifying.

The most frustrating part is dealing with a system where something that is good may not necessarily be rewarded. Hollywood is a machine that needs fuel, a constant regeneration. All you need to do is look at the movies being made today. It's not about quality; it's about feeding the machine and creating two hours of distraction from everyday life. Once you understand that, the frustration lessens. But until you understand the process, it can be very frustrating. You have to keep the light in your life the best you can.

Any further advice?

Don't take a job that you really like, because if you take a job that you don't really care about, it will fuel your ambition. I've seen people take jobs they really like, and it takes up a lot of their time, and they wind up putting their dreams aside. So do something where you can make a living, but not something that will draw you away from what you really want.

WESLEY STRICK

A native New Yorker with a degree in English from the University of California at Berkeley, Wesley worked as a rock critic for magazines such as Rolling Stone, Circus, *and* Creem. *He decided to try his hand at screenwriting after hearing that a friend's screenplay had been sold. His first screenplay,* Final Analysis, *was sold in 1984 to Warner. He eventually penned screenplays for films such as* Cape Fear, True Believer, Arachnophobia, *and* Wolf, *which he cowrote with novelist Jim Harrison.*

How did you begin your career?

I went to college at Berkley. I was an English major. After graduating, I went back to New York and I worked for a few years as a rock critic for all sorts of magazines. A friend I went to Berkley with wrote a screenplay and sold it. It never got made but, at the time, earned him a pretty stunning figure. He told me that if I had any talent as a storyteller, I would get work.

After we got done talking, I went into a bookstore and bought a book called *Screenplay,* by Syd Field. I read it to get the format down. Now I had to think of what to write about. I had a friend, Robert Berger, who ran the prison ward at Bellevue. He always had a lot of fascinating stories, so I asked him to help me find a concept. He came up with a syndrome called pathological intoxication. After that, he told me whatever I needed to know and I began writing.

I sold the screenplay and it was eventually made into a very flawed movie called *Final Analysis,* with Richard Gere, Kim Basinger, and Uma Thurman. At the time, I worked as a word processor for a life insurance company and I would write the script when no one was watching. That took me three to four months. Then I sent the script to my friend in L.A., who gave it to his agent. She took me on as her client. I decided to move to L.A. for at least two years to better understand the business which, at the time, seemed very mysterious.

The second thing I did was a project that was in its very early stages. It became *True Believer* with James Woods. That's basically how I got started.

125

WESLEY STRICK

When you write a script, do you envision particular actors in specific parts?

Sometimes. It helps you get specific with the character.

What is your opinion of film schools?

Never having gone to film school, I really can't answer that. I was an English major, and then I had eight years of menial jobs.

Do you feel it is important to write every day?

For me it is. There are writers who can wait until the last minute, but for me it's important every day. I am very businesslike. I work from 8:30 A.M. to 5:00 P.M., Monday through Friday. I tend to do my best work in the morning. In the afternoon, I usually edit what I've done, or return phone calls or schedule meetings. Sometimes I'll get up in the middle of the night and will stay up and just write dialogue in my head.

What is your relationship with the producer?

Producers—there are all kinds. There are producers you align yourself with, who are powerful and can get movies made. The best of them know that they're not writers. They may give you ideas, but they'll also give you the room to make the ideas work. Then they have a "tango" with the studio. The best producers, in my view, are the ones who know how to get the studio off your back.

Why are other writers brought in for rewrites?

Actors and directors come on the picture with their own anxieties and requirements. The original writers may have been working on the thing for several years, and they're burnt out. Maybe a certain scene, or a new approach, is needed. Sometimes it's easier for an outsider to come in and take a fresh look. One of the reasons I like rewrites is because by the time they hire you, they've been knocking their heads against a wall for a year or more, reading and rereading the material. They get punchy. They don't know what's right or wrong with it anymore. Then you come in and the problems are very clear because it's new.

What is your relationship with the director?

I've done very well with directors. The key is to be collaborative, not to protect every word, idea or scene in your script. You have to acknowledge the reality of Hollywood: the director is the filmmaker—you are not. You are simply the screenwriter and it's a limited position: you are there to serve the director, for better or worse.

Have you ever thought of becoming a director?

Sure. It's funny, though. There are studios hiring new directors simply because they're cheaper and easier to control.

When you are in the process of writing a script, do you let others read the unfinished work?

Yes…a few people—my wife, for one. I feel it's important to let people read it. But before you even write a word, I feel the greatest task, which no one *wants* to do because it's painful and it reveals all the weaknesses in your story, is to sit down and tell your story to your husband, wife, girlfriend, boyfriend, or good friend. Try to hold their attention. If you see their eyes glazing, you know you have a problem. If you have a good story and it's ready to be a screenplay, you should be able to tell it, without stumbling, in twenty minutes.

Where do you get your ideas?

I think there are things in the air that everyone is thinking or talking about that just filter in.

In the face of rejection, how do you maintain a sense of security?

Security is both emotional and financial. The key financially is to not live beyond your means. Emotionally, it's just to keep working…that's my salvation. Even though I'm doing alright now, things go wrong every day. I do get irritated. In my case, I just go back to my computer and keep writing.

What do you find is the most frustrating and then the most gratifying part of being a screen-writer?

The most frustrating is how few movies get made. It's a miracle that anything gets produced—what with how long it takes, how much "blood" gets spilled, how much sweat, how many times you're asked to write and rewrite and rewrite and rewrite. It's like being a marine: you just grit your teeth and do it. And you do it knowing the odds are that you'll never get it on the screen.

The most gratifying part is working with the better directors. I've been lucky enough to work with the likes of Martin Scorsese and Tim Burton. To me, it's like being around royalty. It's also gratifying to see your movie on that big screen and feel the audience's response. It's wonderful to hear their

WESLEY STRICK

laughs, or shouts, or whatever the emotions are that you managed to evoke from your computer a year earlier…that's pretty cool.

What suggestions can you give with regard to obtaining representation?

It's tough. I had the good fortune of knowing someone who knew someone. I do believe that if you have a really good story to tell, somehow it'll get into the right hands. Perseverance is a must! But even more importantly, you have to have the goods.

At this stage of your career, what are your greatest challenges?

To make the transition to directing. As a writer, I have already worked with many of the best directors, so I don't know where else to go except to directing my own work.

Any further advice for an aspiring screenwriter?

You have to write and keep writing—not just one script, but two, three and four. Study structure and Hollywood film grammar—also, great literature. Get inside the craft—to the depth, the essence of the story.

JAMES TOBACK

James attended college at Harvard, where he studied English, and originally planned to write novels; instead, he began writing scripts. He has been nominated for an Academy Award for his brilliant script, Bugsy. *He has also written and directed such films as* Fingers, The Pick Up Artist, *and* The Big Bang.

How did your career begin?

I wrote *The Gambler* "out of the blue." I hadn't thought of making movies at all and started *The Gambler* as a novel. But about halfway through, it dawned on me that I was seeing and hearing it as a movie. So I shifted gears and wrote it as a script. I knew I wasn't ready to direct, so I sent the script to my literary agent who gave it to Mike Medavoy who gave it to Karel Reisz, the British Director, who took to it and spent six months with me preparing it. I was with the movie everyday and rewrote while we were shooting.

From then on, I felt that I should direct everything I wrote. So I wrote and directed my next five movies and would have directed *Bugsy*, which I wrote, but I couldn't because I didn't own it. Warren Beatty had hired me to write it, so it was his decision. In the long run, it went so well. I'm glad he went the way he did—I love the man who directed it (Barry Levinson). The movies I wrote and directed were *Fingers, Love and Money, The Exposed, The Pick Up Artist,* and *The Big Bang.*

Did education have a bearing on what you do today?

No. I didn't really know what I was going to do when I got out of Harvard. I certainly didn't plan on doing movies. I did study English at Harvard, and I wanted to be a writer. But I thought I was going to write novels. Most education gears you to the role of critic more than artist.

What is your opinion on film schools?

Obviously they've worked for certain people. At their very best, they're good for technique and experience. But the very idea of a film "school" suggests that film is removed from, if not divorced from, life—which is precisely what's wrong with most movies today.

JAMES TOBACK

Where do you derive your ideas?

From experience, from life. Even in the case of an historical character like Bugsy Siegel, I wrote him to be a large degree from inside. His character reminded me of a quote from Baudelaire, the French poet and critic. I was drawn to the period, too, and studied the world—the world of my parents and grandparents. And of course, I knew him (Warren Beatty) well and wrote that for him. So Bugsy sprang from different sources.

How do your characters evolve from your basic concept?

I start with the character first, usually a character whose life epitomizes certain themes: sex, love, madness, crime and death—my home ground. Then I let that character lead me wherever he likes.

Is it important for a beginning writer to write everyday?

Probably. It helps to exercise the muscle. But the important thing is confidence. If you don't have confidence, you are lost—no matter how talented you are. You have to feel that you know what you are doing, that you have some significant claim on people's attention.

Do you write your scripts with a specific actor in mind?

It's easier for me if I do. If not, it's necessary to rewrite and adjust the role, although rewriting is integral to all moviemaking.

When you are in the process of writing, do you let anyone read an unfinished draft?

No. I don't even like to read an unfinished draft myself. In some sense, no draft is ever "finished," so sooner or later you have to let the baby out of the cradle.

What are the essential skills a writer needs to get started?

A great imagination, the ability to execute, a good ear for language, and a sense of the world and ideas. You have to accept the fact that failure and humiliation are part of life.

How important is it for the director to understand acting?

Essential. And the process never ends. I am learning more and more with each film. Certain actors don't need a director. They come to the set armed with their performance. They might be terrific even when the director just shuts up and stays aside. Other actors need a lot of provocation, guidance, and help. The relationship between the director and the actor is always personal and specific and particular. All generalities in this area should be viewed with harsh suspicion.

Being both a writer and director, what are the gratifying and then the frustrating parts to both professions?

The most frustrating and longest part is the actual writing. I am always eager to get on with the process of making the movie. You do whatever it takes to fulfill your vision.

Can you suggest helpful books or classes for beginners?

No. I would just say that it helps to have an interesting life. Keep your ears and eyes open around you all the time. Be a good observer and see a lot of films. Find something that you want to write about—something you can't get off your mind.

At this stage of your career, what are your greatest challenges?

To keep writing and directing...to keep finding characters and themes that are exciting, challenging, and true, and to be able to execute them.

What further advice would you give an aspiring writer or director?

Write something you know well. Write about a subject and character you know better than anyone else and stake your claim to that territory. If it excites you and you are familiar with it, envision it and then transcribe your vision. See who should be in it and what it should feel like. Follow your moments of revelation. Stay on the right track.

DANIEL WATERS

Daniel Waters' first original screenplay was the grim, but darkly comedic portrait of teen angst entitled Heathers, *which starred Winona Ryder and Christian Slater. Daniel's other screenwriting credits include the films* Batman Returns, The Adventures of Ford Fairlane, Hudson Hawk, *and recently,* Demolition Man, *with Sylvester Stallone and Wesley Snipes.*

How did your career begin?

I have always wanted to be a writer. It was not until I was twelve and saw the movie *Jaws* that I realized I wanted to write films. I never went to film school, but I did partake in an outstanding screenwriting course while at McGill University in Montreal. I immediately came out to Los Angeles not knowing anything at all, which was a good thing. Being naive was a plus for me, because if I had any idea of the reality of becoming a screenwriter, I probably would have had a stroke.

I got a stressless day job at a video store that allowed me to write at night. Slowly but surely, I ached out my first original screenplay, *Heathers*. The basic step of any screenwriting career is getting one person other than yourself to read and like what you have created. I showed my script to my roommates, who in turn, gave it to their friends. A couple of those friends had agents. One of those agents happened to love the script. The rest is quasi-history.

Where do you get your ideas?

I suck out ideas from everywhere—from the news, from my dreams, from the expression on a strange woman's face sitting in an airport lounge. I don't believe you should be limited to the cliché "write what you know," because it would mean I could only write movies about grouchy screenwriters with rapidly developing potbellies. Writing should be an excuse to seek out and conquer themes that have always fascinated you. If you write only to please other people or to

DANIEL WATERS

sell something for a lot of money, you are going to fail. Please yourself. My main rule is that one should constantly be trying to write "the greatest movie ever made."

What is your opinion of film schools?

I am not a fan, but some people need a push to get out there and write. Film school can allow you to fall down and get back up and have a support group—which can be a nice thing. Also, it is very important to learn the technical basics of a screenplay. If someone wrote *The Godfather* and it was in the wrong format with a lot of typos, no one in the city—absolutely no one—would read it.

Most film schools have a very drab and mundane worship of *structure*. Everything is "Your lead character must do a certain action by a certain page or else!" Yikes! They make screenwriting sound like Math. Little things like innovative plotting and crackling dialogue are disregarded. But then those are the things that can never be taught, and hence, those are the things that separate an interesting screenwriter from a drab and mundane one.

Do you write everyday?

If you need a regiment to write, then you are not a writer. I am the "Anti-Regiment King." I don't believe in enforcing schedules on myself. It's like sitting on the toilet when you don't have to go to the bathroom, which is an apt metaphor considering some of the screenplays I have done. I will sometimes go three days without writing a comma. Then I'll go into twenty straight hours where I don't leave my desk. I am constantly thinking about what I am going to write, even when I am standing in a bank line. So it feels like I do write everyday.

What happened after **Heathers?**

When it came to getting made, *Heathers* was by no means a slam dunk. The script was sent around to everyone in town, and it got vividly and awesomely favorable responses. But when I would say "Great! When do we start shooting?" it would be explained to me that while people admired the writing, no one really wanted to make something that dark, violent, and satirical.

However, from doing this screenplay and not knowing if it was going to sell, I was offered a potpourri of rewrite jobs. I would tell people to just write a good script. Even if no one has the courage to buy it, you will be noticed and people will want to work with you. Your name will go on a list of "Talented People To Be Exploited." By happy fluke, *Heathers* was made by a small studio, New World Pictures.

136

How do your characters evolve from basic concepts?

This may not make sense, but I always tell people to never start writing a script until you are finished with the script—this is to say, before you start staring into a humming computer screen, you should have everything mapped out, you should think out the actions and motivations of your characters from beginning to end. You should spend time stockpiling major character traits and amusing little idiosyncrasies weeks before you type your first word. That way you are going into war with lots of ammunition.

Do you ever have a particular actor in mind when you begin a new script?

I try to shy away from such a thing, and I think actors actually appreciate that. I knew Danny DeVito was going to play the Penguin in *Batman Returns,* so I completely wrote every line with the thought of "What would DeVito say?" When Danny DeVito read the script, he complained that it was too much like his other roles. Actors want a great, original part that they can climb into. They want the challenge.

What is the most frustrating and then the most gratifying part of being a screenwriter?

There is not enough room in the book to address the "Most Frustrating" question. It is amazing how a screenwriter must continually reinvent an "Enthusiastic Naiveté" each time you sit down to write. One cannot avoid the sad truth that the screenplay is only one leg of the relay race, and boy, does the baton get dropped a lot on the way to the finish line.

One likes to think the finished screenplay will be treated like a sacred text, not to be touched. It just doesn't work that way. A nuance you spent months refining to perfection can be completely annihilated in the blink of a director's eye. And then you get the joy of hearing some idiot film critic blame you for a problem that you solved in the screenplay that was botched in the making of the finished film: "The director is a genius, if only he had a decent script to work with." As if the director has nothing to do with the way a script is handled! People should have to read the script if they are going to play the blame game. People who want to be screenwriters always blame the screenplay when they do not like the film; people who are screenwriters know to never blame the screenplay.

The most gratifying part is finishing your script by yourself, reading it over by yourself, and then liking it. It's a private moment that can't be taken away from you. The ugly changes come later.

DANIEL WATERS

What is your relationship with the producer/director?

Many screenwriters, once they turn in the script, are thrown down through a trapdoor, never to be heard from again. I have been fortunate to be able to maintain a close relationship with the directors of my films. That said, the position of the screenwriter on the set is rarely creative. You really have to know your place and pick your battles very sparingly. There are times when you are sitting in dailies and you have to be extremely careful about what you say, for it is a fragile and nervous time for everyone. You must swallow all negativity. The postproduction process can be another story. I have been allowed to let my hair down in the editing room and let loose with brutally constructive criticism. But during filming, you are either a cheerleader or you are fired.

When faced with rejection, how do you maintain a sense of security?

If we lived in our world where every film that was released was great, rejection would be a hard thing to deal with. As it is, the studios make so much pandering-to-the-crowd-and-failing junk, that one can comfort oneself by saying, "Oh well, if that is the kind of garbage they want to make, then no wonder they won't make my script." Screenwriters are brilliant at rationalization. Fortunately (or maybe I should say 'unfortunately') everything I have written has been made. One cannot deny a big luck factor when it comes to whether your screenplay is accepted or rejected.

How important is it to be in Los Angeles versus New York?

New York is the most intense and stimulating city in the world and L.A. is a big, lazy and hazy "mall" that rarely inspires anything. That said, you absolutely have to live in L.A. to be a screenwriter. The New York film scene is a barely existent joke. L.A. is where everything happens whether you like it or not. It is a place where millions of people can accidentally read your script and do something about it. Once you become a screenwriter-god, like Robert Towne or Neil Simon, you can go to Sri Lanka and write scripts. But just starting out, it's L.A., L.A., L.A.

What suggestions can you give in regard to obtaining an agent?

You are going to need luck and have to get to L.A. before you start creating luck. Selling a screenplay from Minnesota isn't luck, it's a miracle. Most agents won't read an unsolicited script, no matter how persistent you are. So you have to start making connections. A "connection" doesn't mean a prominent agent's phone number. It means finding out your friend's ex-girlfriend's brother is an assistant to an agent and getting the script to the agent that way. Again, it all comes down to writing something eye-popping, original, and unique, then getting a person outside of yourself to like it and building from there. Eventually, no matter how convoluted the route, the script will get to an agent.

At this stage of your career, what are your greatest challenges?

My first screenplay, *Heathers,* sprung completely unassisted from my brain. It was an immensely satisfying, creative experience, and yet it remains my only completely original screenplay. I found myself suddenly on a big budget-big movie rollercoaster of dazzling rewrite jobs that I have only recently been able to get off of. I got trapped in an absurd, "failing upwards" trajectory. *Heathers* got me work on a bigger film called *Ford Fairlane.* When that movie failed, I was given a post on an even bigger film, *Hudson Hawk.* After that one really, really failed, I was rewarded with the assignment of *Batman Returns.* Through it all, I really just wanted to go back to writing personal, infinitely-less-glamorous originals.

When I came out here, I took that little video store job because I did not want to get distracted from my writing. In getting a "career" job, a would-be screenwriter moves away from what he or she really wants to do, and that is to write. I came to realize that I had missed the point of my own sermon. By taking the high-paying "career" job of doing blockbuster screenplay assignments, I had moved away from the kind of from-the-heart writing I had come out to do in the first place. My challenge is to get back to the unfettered mind-set that allowed me to create *Heathers.* Wish me luck.

DIRECTORS

TONY BILL

After receiving degrees in both English and Art at Notre Dame, Tony Bill began his career in the film industry as an actor, first starring opposite Frank Sinatra in Come Blow Your Horn *(1963). But he wanted to become a filmmaker, not a movie star. He made his transition to producer with* Deadhead Miles *(1971), followed by* Steelyard Blues *(1973). His next feature,* The Sting *(1973), brought him an Academy Award for Best Picture. Tony has gone on to direct and produce such films as* True Corners *and* Untamed Heart, *and has directed such films as* My Bodyguard *(in which he made his directorial debut),* Six Weeks, A Home of Our Own, *and several others. Since 1974, his Market Street Productions has been called "the closest film-making equivalent of an artists' colony you can find in the movie capital of the world."*

How did you get started in your career?

I started as an actor, and I came to Los Angeles to get a summer job as an actor right out of college. The job I got was starring in a movie with Frank Sinatra, called *Come Blow Your Horn.*

Do you think film school is essential for a person considering a career as a director?

Actually, I discourage people from going to film school. I think it's too much of a hothouse environment. I think that you should get an education...a real education. I mean, there is so much more that needs to be brought to the table by a director than what film school teaches. Given a finite amount of time, one is served better in other ways. If I could be in charge of giving out director's ratings, I would require that you get an acting rating and a producing rating before you were to get a director's rating.

Would you suggest a drama course or theater arts course in college?

No. What I would encourage people to do in college would be to pursue their interest, not what they think is going to get them ahead in life. If you are interested in the theater, great. But if you are only interested in theater as a means to an end, I would discourage that. I don't see education

TONY BILL

as a means to an end or as a tool or as a calling card or even a credential. I see it as an exploration of an interest that one has. So if you are interested in theater, great—but I think people's lives are better served by getting an education. I feel you need to follow your heart.

What do you look for when choosing a project?

I hope to be surprised. I don't look for anything specific.

What is the most frustrating and then the most gratifying aspect of being a director?

The most frustrating is looking for something you want to spend a year or two of your life pursuing...looking for that script that would make you want to spend that amount of your life concentrating on it.

The most rewarding thing is having it turn out well. When I say "well," I don't mean it turns out successfully, or even financially. I mean in the sense that you had a good time doing it, and the year or two of your life you spent doing it brought you to new places or introduced you to new people. It's important to come as close as you can to doing what you thought you wanted to do.

How would you define the director's role?

Well, in my book, I guess the best definition I know of directing was given by Orson Welles, who said: "It's the person who presides over the accidents." I think that is a pretty good description. Either you are presiding over accidents over which you have no control, or you are presiding over the accidents you create. One way or the other, I think that's the job.

How much rehearsal do you feel is necessary?

In general, I don't like to rehearse at all. If some actor or non-actor needs to rehearse, then I will begrudgingly go ahead and rehearse. But generally, I try and avoid it as much as possible. I think for actors it is debilitating, and for non-actors it's a waste of time. I work a lot with non-actors and I don't like to rehearse them either.

How important is it for a director to understand acting?

I think that it is very important. If I were in charge of allowing directors to work, they would first have to pass the acting test. I think that until you are an actor, working as an actor, you will have a hard time communicating with them. Now, some directors do a good job without communicating with their actors, but I don't recommend it as a first choice of how to work.

What is your relationship to the producer/screenwriter?

Well, everyone on the movie is the same. I want to know what they think, how they feel about the direction that the movie is going in. So it's the same with the producer and writer. I enjoy having them on the set. I prefer having the producer and writer on the set at all times. I'd rather make a decision based on their input and their approval and/or lack of approval (whichever it is), but I would like to know about it at the time. If the producer thinks something I am doing is crazy, I would rather know about it while I am doing it than sit in the editing room and find out that he/she was on the set and saw a disaster heading my way and didn't tell me. I can always choose to ignore the advice, but I would rather have it right then and there.

How involved are you in casting?

I am involved one-hundred percent. You generally don't meet everybody possible. You generally only meet people the casting director liked the most. Again, to meet everyone possible would wear you out.

Have you ever directed children?

A lot. I directed a movie with six children!

What is the difference between directing children as opposed to adults?

You have to have a lot of patience, and you have to break the rules of directing a lot by acting their part out for them and telling them how to do it. You have to be specific about how to read a line. It's always fun.

What are the rules when casting children?

I like to say there are no rules when you are directing a child. There are, however, certain child protection laws you have to obey, like different times staying on the set, depending on their age or sometimes depending on what state you are shooting in.

TONY BILL

At this stage of your career, what are your biggest challenges?

Finding something else I want to do after I am finished with what I'm doing is one of the biggest challenges. Pleasing myself is probably the biggest challenge...it's the impossible challenge, actually. The closer I come the better I like it.

Would you like to do any more acting?

It's easy to say "No, I don't want to," but that would keep a closed door on ever doing it again. I have not been interested for the last twenty-five years in making my living as an actor.

When did you stop acting?

Shampoo was about fifteen years ago. I stopped acting for a living when I started producing, which was in the late sixties. I produced *The Sting, Going in Style, Hearts of the West.* I directed *Five Corners, Untamed Heart* and *Six Weeks.*

Is there someone you've tried to emulate or that you have admired?

No, not really. I have tried to do it my way. I moved here to Venice twenty years ago and I have stayed here. I don't think I would trade my life with anyone that I know of.

How closely do you work with the cinematographer?

I like working very closely with the cinematographer. I like to give him a lot of freedom, however. It is hard to get used to for some of them, not being told where to put the camera and how to stage the scene. I try to ask what they think and also be very collaborative.

As a producer, how involved are you in distribution and marketing?

Quite involved. I get involved in the trailer and advertising art and the ad campaign. National distribution is something I don't know or care enough about to get involved in.

Have you ever directed and produced the same film?

Yes, *Five Corners* and *Untamed Heart,* although I did each of them with another producer.

What are the essential skills someone would need to become a director?

I think patience is the most important skill. I think to be a good director, you should know acting and producing. You should have a sense of calmness...you can't fly off the handle at people or yourself. Grace under pressure is important because there is a lot of pressure.

As a producer, how do you decide who you want to be in a film?

Instinct. Whatever makes sense. Maybe some actors you may have liked that you have seen before, or actors that have never acted before. You make a calculated decision. It usually takes a long time. You don't usually get the first person you think of and that's probably just as well. You usually go through quite a few people to find the right person at the right time. You really don't know—you just hope they turn out as good as you had hoped they would.

As a producer, how do you select a director?

It's a matter of the right place at the right time. If you have someone who is unknown, maybe you give them a shot. If you think you need someone famous, then go for them. It's arbitrary and very subjective.

What advice would you give someone whether they wanted to act, direct, or produce?

Watch out that you don't want too much too soon. You might get it. It could be probably the worst thing that could happen to you. I've seen more people's lives harmed by getting too much than too little.

When you are faced with rejection, how do you maintain a sense of security?

I don't. I just keep going, despite the fact that I don't feel good about it.

Have you directed television?

A few pilots...a few TV movies. It's just twice as fast to work.

Do you have any advice with regard to obtaining representation?

There is no easy road. Everyone has to find their own way. Have perseverance—that's the number-one key. I've never seen anyone persevere and not succeed.

ROB BOWMAN

Rob Bowman's first directing experience was doing "inserts" for The A-Team *and several other Stephen Cannell shows. Since then he has directed more than seventy television shows such as* Stingray, Star Trek: The Next Generation, Quantum Leap, Parker Lewis Can't Lose, Midnight Caller, *and* Hat Squad. *He recently completed his first feature film,* Airborne, *for Mel Gibson's Icon Productions.*

How did you begin your career?

My career began its practical course through the Paramount Studios/Stephen J. Cannell Productions mailroom. Yesiree! Humble beginnings they were...but beginnings, nonetheless. I wanted to direct, but had no film to show my wares. So it was off to the copy machine to practice my art. "Surely the careers of DeMille, Coppola, Ford—even Spielberg—must have started this way," I told myself daily. Career anxiety, stress, is measured by the distance between where you are now and where or who you'd like to be someday. For me, tomorrow would be fine, but that was not to be so.

I had to be patient, wait my turn, educate myself in night classes on the aesthetics, story structure, and whatever else I could learn about film between 7 and 11 P.M., Monday through Friday. Lo and behold, one day there was an insert to be shot on two different episodes at the exact same time. I had been doing my best at copying and delivering those darn scripts and also helping out the insert department, now and then, and Mr. Cannell graciously allowed me to shoot my first insert.

A start it was! If you practice enough, you get better. I did so. Cannell gave me my first full episode of television. I haven't stopped since then. I'm also available for home or office copy machine repair. Remember, check your toner before each usage.

Is attending film school essential?

For some, yes; not for all. I have friends who attended film school but did not gain entry into the business from film school knowledge, but from who they met at film school. Friends help friends in this business because they have a trust that builds up, and also because they want to work with people they enjoy working with. If film school offers a way to unlock the passion you need to be an artist and you have no other foreseeable way to practice, learn, then gain entry, then go. I believe ultimately you have to be ready when an opportunity presents itself to to you. Knowledge is power, so we must educate ourselves one way or another if we plan to stay around.

What skills should a director have?

The language of the camera: what each lens can do for you—angle, camera height…all which deal with the language of the camera. Writing skills are essential to best create and interpret screenplays. People skills: you must be able to work with people to get what the film needs out of each person working on it. Editorial skills: this is where you can make or break your movie.

This is a tough question because a director needs to know about everything. The trick is working while you don't know enough. You've got to be decisive and quick, even if you're not sure. Decide! That's why you're there: to be the decision-maker.

Is it important for a director to understand acting?

Yes. If you want the actor to confide in you during the process of shooting, then you must understand what the problems are of finding the moment or defining the character. When they have questions, you can help them find the answers. If you have an idea for a character, you're going to be better received if you can speak to the actor in a way that he or she understands. More efficient, less takes, better film.

What is the director's relationship with the producer and the screenwriter?

Since the producer in one way or another is the money-dispenser, this relationship is interesting because his or her job is to spend the money intelligently; my objective is to make the best picture possible, and at many times these two don't go together. The relationship with the screenwriter in feature films is very close during preproduction. If you can both deliver to the screen what it was you originally intended, then the job is well done. The director and screenwriter both bring their visions to the table and must then mold them into one.

What do you look for when choosing a project?

A studio that will hire me! No, seriously, this is another difficult problem. How do you choose material that deals with what you have to say, will allow you to flourish as the filmmaker you are, but the world doesn't yet know about, and all the while getting the job in the first place? I'm at a place in my career where I'm being handed several scripts, most of which would be considered "mainstream" or "low risk" material. Only if the script I would choose of these makes money at the box office would it further my chances of doing a riskier, more personal film. Well, box office is largely controlled by the marketing campaign and through audience awareness of the film. If the audience doesn't know about your film, they won't go see it. It has nothing to do with your film or what a splendid filmmaker you may actually be. Your success lies in the course of Friday, Saturday, and Sunday box office reports. Go figure. What to do? Answer: make films people want to see. No problem. Which script is it of the pile sent to you? Answer: pick the script that you enjoy and could become passionate about, and your voice will come through the film on the screen and into the hearts and minds of the audience.

Did you have a mentor?

Yes, and they are forever alive in my mind. Not to imply that any have moved on to the next dimension, but that they are always talking to me in my head. My father, Chuck, Howard Anderson III, Stephen Cannell, Frank Lupo, Roy Huggins were all the first and still the most significant and influential mentors...so far.

How much rehearsal is necessary when preparing for a film?

Rehearsal varies for each project. This depends on the cast and the script. Two weeks? Six weeks? Enough to blend the cast into the pallet you need.

What is the most frustrating and then the most gratifying part of being a director?

The most frustrating moment of making a film, for me, is the first assembly of the film, also known as the "first cut." Gratifying is seeing people cheer, laugh, cry, sit on the edge of their seats—all the things that add up to the ultimate reason we're here: to entertain.

At this stage of your career, what are your greatest challenges?

Keeping my house from the bank. Actually, it's the continual growth in my assignments...projects that stretch me and invigorate me...that wonderful kinetic sense of fresh material breezing by my eyes. Good material is hard to find. And once you've proven your talents and your worth, along with endurance and a good batting average, so every timeout is (is) the last show you'll ever direct, you want to make it your best. Meeting A-list filmmakers and getting a new, more powerful mentor must be my next step.

Any further advice?

Stick to it. My advice is that you better be ready to find out some hard truths about yourself, because when you're new and young in this business, you're going to pay for your opportunity to be here. And if you don't love it, you won't make it. If you do love it and you do make it, there is nothing sweeter than listening to a darkened theater, full of people watching your movie, as they laugh and cry and cheer and applaud when the credits roll.

JAMES BRIDGES

A former actor, James Bridges continued his career through writing and eventually directing. His film credits include The Paper Chase, The China Syndrome, Urban Cowboy, *and* Bright Lights, Big City.

Would you briefly explain how you got started in your career?

I was a drama major with a music minor and an English minor at Arkansas State Teacher's College. I decided to come to California to become an actor. I attended the Pasadena Playhouse Starfinder Session in 1956, and I won the award that summer as the most promising student. And with that came a part on the Matinee Theater, which was a television show that was done by NBC every day at 12:00 noon. I got an agent out of that, and I did fifty television shows and seven features as an actor.

I then went away to the service, and when I came back there was no work. So I started to write. I wrote a play that was done at the Beverly Hills Playhouse with Jan Sterling and Dennis Hopper. From the play I became a writer on the Hitchcock show [*Alfred Hitchcock Presents*].

Out of the Hitchcock show, I started writing features. I wrote three or four features, then decided I wanted to direct and I started to direct. Oddly enough, it was very smooth. There were a lot of tough days not working, but it was very smooth. It just sort of all molded together.

Do you think film school is essential for a person pursuing a career as a director?

It certainly was not essential when I started because there weren't that many film schools, and the people that were coming out of film schools everybody felt were pretentious. But now that so many people in the industry are out of film school and since the explosion of the directors—George Lucas, Francis Ford Coppola, Steven Spielberg—all those people came out of film school, now I would think a lot of people feel you have to go. I don't think it's absolutely essen-

JAMES BRIDGES

tial. I think there are several problems in film schools, that they don't really relate to audiences the way they should. They don't work with the theater department. So you can learn a lot technically, and anything you can learn about the film business is good, obviously, but I would say it's not absolutely essential.

How would you define the role of the director?

I'm a writer/director, so what happened to me was I felt that the films that I was writing and what I was seeing in my mind was not getting on the screen. So I wanted to be an "auteur," which was a chic word at that time. But a director is really responsible for all that. In television it's very interesting because I did so much work in television. Producers and writers do the show. But in film, at least during the time that I was making most of my films, the director was the most important person. Now that the studios have tried to take the power away from the director, they hire first-time directors or directors they know they can handle. The *real* director is responsible for everything.

What is the director's relationship to the cinematographer?

I think it's—next to the actor—the most important relationship on a movie. I've been very fortunate to work with two of the greatest in the world: Gordon Willis, who shot *Paper Chase* for me; and Ray Villalobos, who shot *Urban Cowboy* for me. That relationship is so essential. The cinematographer has to understand the director's vision. You have to spend a great deal of time working on what I call the "pallet" of the movie. You have to decide what the film is going to look like, what the colors are going to be, whether you're going to use nets or any kind of flashing. You have to work with this person to make a smooth relationship on the set. He's very much a part of the storytelling.

How important is it for the director to understand acting?

I think it's very important. I was an actor myself in the beginning. I can tell, when I go see a movie, a film that is directed by someone who knows something about acting or who has been an actor themselves. Several years ago when I took *Paper Chase* to a broadcaster in New York, we showed it to a college. A student came up afterward and said: "How can I become a director? What should I do?" And I said: "What are you doing?" He said: "I'm in the film department here." And I said: "Get out of the film department, get into the drama department where you learn how to act, where you learn how to deal with actors, where you learn to play in front of an audience. Because in the film department, you're going to learn a lot of technical stuff that you're going to learn anyway...but it's the other stuff that you need to know."

Is there some one that you tried to emulate in your career?

I admire anybody who gets a film made. But my favorite director, I guess, and the person, if I tried to emulate somebody, would have been Stanley Kubrick. I find him to be certainly one of our greatest directors.

Is there anything in particular that you look for when choosing a project?

I like to make "how to" movies—movies that have more than just a story, but have something else going. *Paper Chase* was how to become a lawyer; the *Urban Cowboy* thing was how to become a contemporary cowboy. I like things that have something unusual. It's very strange...I never really know what's going to appeal to me when I pick up a script, but I do look for things that have a superstructure of some sort.

How much rehearsal do you feel is necessary?

I try to rehearse at least two weeks, if I can. I always want to give myself enough time, in case the script doesn't work, to rewrite it. It also depends on the actors. Some actors don't want to rehearse that long.

What are the most essential skills in becoming a good director?

I think you have to have a will of iron. I think you have to know what you want and to know how to get it. You have to have certain skills for how to deal with people. Of course there are a lot of directors who are very famous for being rough and tough and mean to people, but I find that things work better if you are able to create an atmosphere on a set where people are comfortable and do their best work. I think that's a skill.

What is the most frustrating and then the most gratifying part of being a director?

The most frustrating part now is this market-research, focus-group stuff that all of the studios are now doing. The people who make the movies, besides the ones who are running the studios, really don't love movies the way the people, when I first began, loved the movies. And they don't even really care. All they really care is that they make money. So the most frustrating thing is that you work very hard. And if they can take the movie to this market-research thing, then they want the audience to tell you how to redo the movie—I just find that absolutely frustrating. The most rewarding thing is getting it made and having it be a success.

JAMES BRIDGES

What suggestions can you give with regard to obtaining representation?

I think it's harder to get an agent as a director if you don't have anything done. I guess it's true for an actor, and it would be the same advice that everybody gives. If you're a director, you should try to develop a script—that's how I did it. I developed a script that I knew they wanted to do, and I brought it in. The first thing to know is you're not a director. So I took my income tax return that year and I went to New York and financed a play off Broadway—and I directed a play. It said in *The New York Times* that James Bridges was a director. And then I brought the reviews back and I said, "Here. I'm a director."

At this stage of your career, what is the biggest challenge?

I would like to make a series of films that are more personal...and I guess by that it means that they're less expensive. And by that, I don't know if you can ever get them financed. I would like to make a series of personal films. I would also like to make a science fiction film. I'd like to do a film with more epic proportions in it.

MARSHALL HERSKOVITZ

Marshall Herskovitz hails from Philadelphia and attended Brandeis University, where his studies took a turn toward filmmaking. A short film, In Foot Steps, *won him acceptance to the American Film Institute in 1975. It was during his studies at the American Film Institute that Marshall met his partner Edward Zwick. Marshall and Edward are responsible for developing several projects, including the Emmy Award winning TV movie* Special Bulletin *(for which Marshall was the producer and the coauthor), and the Emmy Award winning TV show* Thirtysomething. *For his work on* Thirtysomething, *Marshall was awarded two Emmys, one for Best Dramatic Series and another for Best Writing in a Dramatic Series. He has also won the Golden Globe award, and recently directed the film* Jack the Bear, *starring Danny DeVito. With Zwick, Marshall has created The Bedford Falls Company as the home of their future film and television projects, one of which is the critically-acclaimed* My So-Called Life.

How did your career begin?

When I graduated from Brandeis University in 1973, I decided I wanted to be a filmmaker. The best way to do that was to make a film. So I took all the money I had and made a forty-minute, color, sixteen-millimeter, sync-sound, dramatic film. Knowing nothing about anything, I borrowed the equipment from the Brandeis film department, and just blundered into it. The film I made turned out to be a complete disaster. So I came out to Los Angeles, and applied to the American Film Institute and eventually got in.

It was a very seminal experience for me. I had two excellent teachers there: Nina Foch and Jan Kadar. Even before I got my first job writing, I wrote an episode of *Family* with a partner. I had a career before I was out of AFI. Although I went through tough times afterward, that's basically how I got started.

Is attending film school essential?

It is not essential, but it is the primary way to get into the business and it is the smartest way.

MARSHALL HERSKOVITZ

Is there another way in, besides attending film school?

Write—you will be hired as a writer quicker than a director.

What are the skills needed by a director?

There are so many different kinds of directors. I am not sure there is one good answer. For example, there are some brilliant directors that have no people skills at all, who people hate, and actors hate. Making films with this type of director can be a miserable experience, but they make brilliant films. And then you have very beloved directors. Some directors have a brilliant eye and are very graphically oriented. Then, for example, some of the old time directors, like George Cukor, had the worst cinematic eye imaginable, but we loved to watch his movies.

I think to be a good director you have to be able to balance things in many different facets. As a director, you have to deal on an emotional level with actors, but also be an artist who looks through a camera and takes pictures. There are a lot of things that I believe in that have nothing to do with other directors. For me, it's a sense of reality. In other words, I am trying to create this illusion of reality. My partner often says it's like trying to stuff nine pounds in a three-pound bag...like bringing things to a scene until it comes to life, has a life of it's own. It feels like something is really happening. So for me, the most essential skill for a director is to be able to do a balancing act.

Does a director have to understand acting?

The absolute answer to that is it's not important at all. We have historical proof. Alfred Hitchcock did not have a clue. There are several living directors (whom I won't name) who are considered by actors to be utterly inhumane and illiterate when it comes to acting. Yet these same directors make movies that work. On the other hand, I think that there are very few great directors who didn't really have a deep understanding of what acting was about and what actors were about and who didn't have a powerful way of communicating with actors even if it wasn't direct. So it's a rule that has several exceptions, but it is a rule.

What is the director's relationship with the producer/screenwriter?

Most of the time, I have been the producer when I am directing. I'm not a good example of that. Although, I think the producer's role should be to support the director. The screenwriter is a more complicated relationship. For me, I started out as a writer and I think of myself as a filmmaker.

When you are a filmmaker, you don't stay in one cubbyhole—you absorb it all. My particular orientation towards directing is that the director is the author of the film. I don't believe that's the only way to make a film, but that's how I work. Therefore, in some way I always reinvent the film when I direct, so my relationship with the screenwriter can either be congenial or difficult, depending on the screenwriter's willingness to be a part of that process. It is one of those situations that is inherently unfair and unbalanced, but it is the only way the system can work. Authorship in movies is not the same as authorship in books. It is a painful reality.

What do you look for when choosing a project?

There is a silly old Miami Beach joke that perfectly conveys my philosophy of choosing material: Mrs. Feingold is redecorating her apartment in Miami Beach and the decorator says, "What period would you like the furnishings?" Mrs. Feingold says, "What is this period?" He says, "You know, Louis the 16th, Regency?" She thinks for a minute and replies, "Listen Sonny, I'll tell you what period I want it in: I want it should be so gorgeous, my friends should come in, take one look and drop dead—period!" So I always say: "I want to do period films."

The idea that when I choose a project, frankly, I say to myself, "This is going to take a year of my life and am I going to be as excited about this at the end of it as I was in the beginning? And is it something I will be proud of? And will it last in people's minds, or will it just be two hours of entertainment?" Most of this business is oriented towards giving people two hours of entertainment. And I have nothing against that, I just don't know how to do it. It's not the way I got into this business. It's really about my own ability to be passionate about what I choose.

Who have you tried to emulate in your career?

I would not use the word "emulate," but there are certain directors who I admire so much that I have thought about them when I do my own work. I am not sure you would see them in my style. The first would be Frank Capra, and that has more to do with how I conceptualize the movies. In other words, it has more to do with me as a storyteller than where I put the camera or how I deal with an actor. But Capra, as a storyteller, had the ability to deal with ambivalence in a way that no one else has come close to, in my experience. A perfect example is *It's a Wonderful Life*. He has had a very strong influence on my philosophy of filmmaking.

MARSHALL HERSKOVITZ

How much rehearsal is necessary?

It depends on the actors. Some actors get worse with rehearsal. What I have found to be very effective is improvisational rehearsal. This is where the actor finds the character within himself. Make up scenes before you start shooting. It helps you as a director, and the actors discover who they really are.

At this stage of your career, what are your greatest challenges?

My greatest challenge is entirely in my own head, and it is simply to find and create material and do it justice.

Any further advice?

Don't do this unless you have no choice. It's too hard and it's not worth it. So you really have to know this is all you can do. The people who end up doing this are people who can't do anything else. It's a very difficult business to break into. It can mess up your head and your life, so you need to know this going in. I don't think it is a glamorous business. So if you are getting into it for the glamour, those are the wrong reasons. The other thing I would say is that if you are a passive person, it's not for you. You have to learn to be persistent and have a strong goal. If you are willing to put up with a lot for a long time, you might be one of the people that will make it.

RANDAL KLEISER

Prior to the release of his first feature film, Grease, *Randal worked in television, directing episodes of* Marcus Welby, M.D., Starsky & Hutch, The Rookies *and* Family, *and the Emmy-Award-winning TV movie* The Gathering, *for which he received a Best Director Emmy nomination. Other feature films to his credit include:* The Blue Lagoon, Flight of the Navigator, Big Top Pee Wee, White Fang, *and* Honey, I Blew Up the Kid. *Randal also serves on the Student Academy Awards Committee of the Academy of Motion Picture Arts and Sciences.*

How did your career begin?

I originally wanted to be a cartoonist for Walt Disney when I was a kid. I took a drive out to Los Angeles with my family when I was twelve years old. I had made a film and wanted to show it to Walt Disney. The guard would not let us in without an appointment. So I went back to Philadelphia.

I decided to give up cartoons to become a live action director. I did eight-millimeter films with my friends, and then I decided I wanted to learn more. So later on, I applied to USC film school. I was accepted and came back out to Los Angeles. At the same time, George Lucas came down from Modesto, California to study film. He and I attended USC the same semester and became friends. I was an actor in his first student film, and he was a cameraman in my first student film. At the time, no students had ever gotten out of film school and gone into directing, because the movie business was still a closed shop. There were no young people directing.

About that time, *Easy Rider* came out and made a lot of money, and suddenly they realized there was a huge market there. Young people were willing to pay a lot of money to see movies about themselves, about their generation and made by directors their age. So suddenly things started to shift, and more and more people started getting jobs. We were slowly starting to infiltrate the film business.

RANDAL KLEISER

I made a student film through USC, and started to direct hour-long shows at Universal—*Marcus Welby, Starsky & Hutch*, and *The Rookies*. Following that, I was given a shot at directing television movies. I directed a film for Robert Stigwood's company. The film was *All Together Now*.

Do you think film school is essential?

It's not essential today, but the advantage of film school is that you can make a film which can then be seen and get discovered. You can make films without film school, working in video. When we went to school, we had to put up a lot of money to get equipment. Today, anybody can pick up a wide camera and make a film, then transfer it to VHS, sit down, and watch it. Somebody in Des Moines who is very clever and very good with very little money—maybe less than $50.00—can make a film. They could launch a career, which never could have happened when I started.

What do you look for when choosing a project?

I'm trying to get out of the pop-culture-type movies and into films about people and how time changes relationships—and adult themes. I'm really avoiding anything about children, animals, fantasy, or teenagers. So that leaves a lot of things out.

Is it important for a director to understand acting?

I think it's essential. In that regard, when I was at USC, I studied acting under Nina Foch. She was a great actor, teacher, and coach. I learned an awful lot about how an actor feels and what they have to go through. When I was in film school, I acted in commercials to get money for my student films. So being in front of the camera, I was able to see the problems an actor can have that you would not know about if you had never done it.

Do you ever take suggestions from actors?

Certainly. You want to always draw from an actor whatever talent that they have to improve the performance. Many times they will have thought out the character very specifically. As long as it's in sync with how I see the character, I enjoy having that collaboration.

What does a director's job entail?

The director is responsible for shaping the telling of the story and determining how it will be told, what type of actor will play it, what kind of clothing he or she will be wearing, whether it will be in widescreen, what kind of music will be playing in the background, whether they are sitting in a chair or walking across the room while they're doing their line. Every detail of the storytelling process is the director's responsibility. On the other hand, the producer hires everybody and handles the finances.

What is your relationship to the producer?

A good producer will hire the best people possible, and then support the director and help him or her if he or she has any problems right away. Otherwise, let the director do the job. Those are the best kind.

Did you have a mentor or someone you tried to emulate?

I've always liked the films of George Cukor. I was able to meet him before he died. Another man whose style I liked a lot is Robert Wise. I liked Jim Bridges, too. I've worked for Jim. I like people who are not screamers, people who are kindly and have integrity.

How much rehearsal is necessary?

It depends on the project. If the actor is playing something very foreign to them, that requires a lot more rehearsal. Or if they're playing something completely opposite, that would require more rehearsal. It depends on the actor.

What are the most frustrating and gratifying parts of being a director?

I think the most frustrating part is when you are shooting, because so many things can go wrong and you have to adapt to them, including outside influences such as weather. Dealing with uncontrollable forces is the most frustrating part.

The most gratifying part is in the editing room, where you start putting your master shots and close-ups together, shaping the movie, watching it come alive—and it works.

What advice can you give someone who is just getting started?

I think the best advice would be to make video projects. Videos that are not trying to imitate, but trying to say something that they feel about life, or about people or a vision that they have of how to see something—anything that comes from within that they can put onto tape that shows a unique way of how they look at things. And make it a short, five-minute tape showing something that people aren't used to seeing—something that's fresh and different. That will help a lot.

RANDAL KLEISER

How does one obtain representation?

Take the tape that I just suggested to agents. That tape should probably have—if they want to be a director for features—a scene that is funny or intense or unusual, with maybe two actors. It should show something that's from the heart of the director.

Are there agents that will see unsolicited material?

That requires an industrious streak. I think the best thing to do would be to spend some time in Los Angeles and just push. You can't expect to just sell your film. You've got to have drive and a personality that is willing to go out and sell. You must be pushy. There are two kinds of pushiness: obnoxious or passionate. Passionate pushy people are the ones who are successful, and obnoxious pushy people are the ones who are not.

At this stage of your career, what is your greatest challenge?

Right now, the greatest challenge is being given the chance to make the kind of films that have some meaning and are about humanity. I've been typed as a "pop director," and even though I made *Getting It Right*, it's hard to get studios to think of me when these quality projects come around.

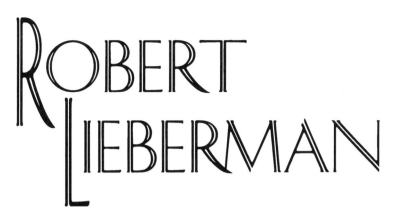

ROBERT LIEBERMAN

Robert Lieberman attended the University of Buffalo and was the first to graduate with a degree in film. Some of his credits include Fire in the Sky, Table for Five *(with Jon Voight),* All I Want for Christmas, *and the television movie* To Save a Child. *He is married to actress Marilu Henner.*

How did your career begin?

I made some student films [at the University of Buffalo], and then was an assistant editor. After that, I became a director of television commercials, which led to television and films.

What is the role of the director?

It varies, certainly, in different mediums. The circumstances in making a film are defined by the people involved, and the director can be anything from a total dictator to just a pawn. It depends what the relationship is between that director and the producer, and the director and the studio. But the basic job of a director is to envision what the film will end up being, and having that vision very complete in his head so he is able to direct all the different crafts involved in the making of a film.

How did education or training affect your career?

The main aspect of education, as it applies to filmmaking, for me, was not the skills I did not learn—how to focus the camera or design a pan or make a dissolve. What my education gave me was an understanding of the aesthetics of film. This is because the business itself does not have any real love for aesthetics. It's truly a business that wants to make money. So it is the director who must retain the artistic vision, and to do so should learn the pure art of the film.

ROBERT LIEBERMAN

Do you think film school is essential?

I don't think it's essential. I think it's valuable. I graduated from film school—the University of Buffalo. As I said earlier, I was the first person to graduate with a degree in film from that institution. What I learned was extremely valuable, but it was not mandatory.

Is it important for a director to understand acting?

That's mandatory. There is no way to direct without understanding acting. A great number of directors don't understand acting, and I think their work suffers for it. It's fundamental. In some television situations many actors are left on their own to protect themselves and figure it out. Television directors are brought in more or less to be policemen...to set up the shots. But in motion pictures, it's very important that a director understand how an actor functions and what that actor needs to deliver a performance.

What are the most frustrating and the most gratifying parts of being a director?

The most frustrating part is having to compromise your vision to businessmen and bureaucrats—people that are not artists nor storytellers—and having to work under the constraints of time and budget.

The most gratifying is when you have a thought in your head one day and six months later you see it fully realized on screen and witness the effect it has on an audience. That's the joy.

What do you look for when choosing a project?

I look for something very personal that interests me a great deal and something the audience will believe in—that's the only criteria.

What skills should a director possess?

You need many skills. The most important skill is understanding human relations, not only because all storytelling involves human drama, but also because the process puts you at the focal point of many different social relationships that have to be understood and nurtured. You have to be the "daddy" on the set as well as the "mommy."

To be a good director you must have an understanding of all the crafts it takes to make a movie. These are the director's tools. The greater the grasp of these various technical skills, the more adept the director will be at realizing his vision. It's like being a conductor in an orchestra: you don't have to play all the instruments, but you have to know how they are played and if they are being played well.

How do you get an agent?

I've been doing this for twenty-two years and have had at least ten different agents, starting with small agencies and eventually to two of the big three. It's difficult to get representation as a director—it's impossible without something to display. No one will hire a young person who desires to be a director just because he or she has a dream. You have to come up through the ranks. It's not a fast process.

The quickest route to being a director is by writing. Write a spec script that a studio wants made and make it contingent upon you being the director—that's the quickest way.

Do you ever take suggestions from actors?

I always keep a running dialogue with the actors. After all, their entire responsibility is to understand the character and that character's behavior.

How much rehearsal do you feel is necessary?

A limited amount—I don't like to overrehearse. Two weeks is about average, just so the actors have an understanding of their characters and I get an idea of what to expect. Otherwise, I'm a big believer in spontaneity.

NANCY MALONE

Born in Queens Village, Long Island, Nancy Malone's career began at age five as a successful child model. She began acting on radio and television, and appeared in several outstanding television programs, including two series: Naked City *and* The Long Hot Summer. *She joined* Tomorrow Entertainment *as Director of Motion Pictures and was instrumental in securing the company's commitment to* Miss Jane Pittman, *winner of nineteen Emmys. Ms. Malone also became the first Vice President of Television at Twentieth Century Fox. She has directed several television shows, including* Dynasty, Knots Landing, Beverly Hills 90210, Cagney & Lacey, Hotel, *and* Melrose Place.

How did you get started in your career?

I got started modeling and acting at age five. Freud would say there are no accidents, so perhaps it was all destiny. While caddying at a country club, my brother Roger, who was nine years my senior, was approached by a man who owned an advertising agency. The gentleman thought Roger had a great face for selling breakfast cereal, orange juice, etc. When my brother told my mom the gentleman's comments, my mother was very reluctant to go to the next step (that being photographs taken by the executive's photographer).

My mother finally decided "yes." Seeing as how she had no one to leave me with, she brought me along to the studio. The photographer thought I had potential as well, took some pictures, and sent my photos along with my brother's to John Robert Powers, who at that time in the '40s was the biggest modeling agent in the world. I was called immediately, and my career took off like a rocket. I became a very successful child model and at the age of ten, I appeared on the cover of *Life* magazine.

I went on to become an actress as well. At fourteen, I appeared on Broadway in my first play, *Time Out for Ginger,* with Melvyn Douglas, and then later on appeared in such plays as: *Major Barbara* with Charles Laughton, *A Touch of the Poet* with Helen Hayes, and *The Chalk Garden* with Judith Anderson. Subsequently, I costarred in a TV series called *The Naked City,* and it was a wonderful experience. I received an Emmy nomination for my performance. Then I came to

NANCY MALONE

Los Angeles and did a pilot for Twentieth Century Fox, *The Long Hot Summer*, based on the Faulkner book and the movie directed by Robert Altman. I did the series, and when the show was completed I guest-starred in most of the leading shows of the time.

As the '70s approached, I seemed to become restless because I couldn't find any fulfilling roles. Tom Moore, former ABC Network President, suggested that I find good material and produce it myself (both of my series were for ABC). Moore was going to start a production company called "Tomorrow Entertainment," and he offered me a job in development. Of course I had to give up my acting career. I took a deep breath and made the decision to do that. I learned a lot and I knew I could go on to produce movies for TV.

After two years, I left Tomorrow Entertainment and opened my own office. I sold a project to NBC, my first two-hour movie. I produced it and it was called *Winner Take All*, with Shirley Jones. It was a success. Twentieth Century Fox Studios called and asked if I would come over and head-up their development department. Eventually, I became the first woman vice president of a major motion picture studio. After getting some shows on the air for Fox, I resigned and produced a few TV movies for CBS. Frustrated by not being able to having more hands-on, I decided that I needed to direct. I then enrolled in the American Film Institute's women's directing program and completed two short films.

After the American Film Institute, I spent a year trying to get a job. An executive saw my short film. Lynn Loring, who at the time was head of Aaron Spelling's company, was very enthusiastic. She in turn showed it to Esther Shapiro, the creator of *Dynasty*, and Elaine Rich, the producer. They both liked it, and I got my first assignment. It was the hundredth anniversary program of *Dynasty*. I have been very lucky and have gone on to direct many other Aaron Spelling shows. Now I am directing *Melrose Place* and hopefully one day I can graduate to features.

Do you think film school is essential?

Judging by my career, I don't think film school is essential. I have known many people that have had great success and have never gone to film school. What I do think is, if you don't have access to a set or people in the industry, film school can be helpful and interesting. Film school for historical as well as technical expertise can be useful. One can also learn a lot by going to movies, or renting movies. It's up to the individual.

Is it important for a director to understand acting?

(*Emphatically*) Yes! As an actress I worked with wonderful directors and terrible directors. It's extremely important for a director to understand the actor's pain and psyche and needs. Every person who wants to be a director should read for a part, try and get it, then go onstage and try to act.

Do you ever take suggestions from actors?

Yes, I do. Sometimes they're wonderful. It all depends on the actors. Some actors don't have a lot of experience and suggest business that doesn't work, but I appreciate the interest. Seeing as how the director must see the show overall, and the actors only see their parts, I try to be sensitive when I have to turn their suggestions down and tell them that it doesn't work. Actors who have a lot of experience will show me exactly what they want to do in the first rehearsal and it's usually right on and just needs shaping.

What does a director's job entail, specifically describing directing for television?

It's very hard to describe exactly what a director's job entails. Perhaps a combination ringmaster, mother, teacher, therapist, timekeeper, interpreter, etc. It requires stamina, goodwill, humor, and an ability to compromise and concentrate. For episodic television, you are given a script, hopefully the day you start your preparation. You read your script and look for locations. You read actors for non-regular parts in the show. You make notes on the characters: where they start and where they are in each act. You draw diagrams of the sets and determine the blocking, camera angle, lenses, equipment. You meet with the producer and the location person and your First A.D. [assistant director]. You have rewrites all the time, so you work with your writers. You use all your prep-time for your seven-day shoot. Generally, it's not enough. If you have a wonderful production manager and First A.D., your assignment can be enjoyable—stressful, but enjoyable.

How does one obtain representation?

I think that's the question everyone asks in Hollywood. You never know. Even if you get representation, is it the right representation for you? The facts speak for themselves. If you get jobs from the agents and they're servicing you, then probably it's the right agent. I don't know anyone happy with their agent. It's very hard to find representation if you're a newcomer. You have to have a piece of film under your arm and you have to be persistent. There is nothing like being persistent. Without being a pain, you have to be persistent. It's a fine line.

NANCY MALONE

Did you have a mentor or someone you tried to emulate?

I had a mentor in Tom Moore, the gentleman who first hired me and encouraged me to have a new career. I never really had the chance to emulate anyone. I would certainly like to follow Oliver Stone around, or Martin Scorsese, but I haven't had that opportunity. There were no women role models when I started. I'm told now that I've become a role model.

Is there anything you look for when choosing a project?

Yes. I look for the "arch" of the story. What does it say? What does it have to do with life? What does it have to do with relationships? What are the conflicts? Are the characters true? Why make this movie? I look for things that have some kind of mystery. Stella Adler, my acting teacher, used to say, "The best actors have secrets." I always feel that way about stories. What's the underlying secret between the characters?

What is the most frustrating and then the most gratifying part of being a director?

The time element is the most frustrating. That means there is next to no rehearsal and I believe strongly in rehearsal. The most gratifying part of being a director is when you give an actor a direction and the actor gets it and makes it his or her own.

What suggestions can you give to someone just starting out?

See all the great old films. Look through libraries. See what pictures won Academy Awards. Go to the classics and look at them, feel them, study them. Look at the angles the director chose. Memorize. Figure out why you had certain reactions to certain films. These things are very important in your development and part of your tool box. That would be my best advice.

At this stage of your career, what is the biggest challenge?

My greatest challenge is to stay in the business. It has changed terribly. Also, to continue to be turned on to good stories, to be inspired by good acting.

JEFF MARGOLIS

Jeff Margolis has been a producer/director for the past twenty-three years. He has directed The Academy Awards *for the last six years, and* The American Music Awards *for the last thirteen years. His other credits include* The Miss America Beauty Pageant, Oscars' Greatest Moments, Richard Pryor Special, *and* A Gala for the President at Ford's Theater. *Jeff is also an Emmy Award Winner.*

Can you tell me how you got started in directing?

I actually went into college as a pre-med student. After one semester, I decided that I wasn't really doing this because I wanted to...I was doing this because my parents wanted me to do it. Since I always had a love of television—especially variety shows—I knew this was what I really wanted to do, and I woke up one morning, looked in the mirror and changed my major.

What did your parents say?

They weren't thrilled, but they were very supportive.

How did you then prepare yourself?

I went to USC and I was in film school and I decided to transfer over to the UCLA Theater Arts Department, because back then they had a larger television department. As I was going to school, I got a job doing cue cards. I did two shows a week: *Let's Make a Deal* and *The Smothers Brothers Comedy Hour.* Whenever I wasn't really busy, I would break away to watch the director and producer work. I was fascinated by it. I continued the cue cards for about six months for this one company, and then left and opened my own company which gave me a lot more time to sit in control booths and editing rooms and listen and learn.

JEFF MARGOLIS

Can you explain how education had a bearing on what you do today?

Well, I think it's important to get an education. I think on-the-job training is much more beneficial. It was for me. I learned much more on the stage and in the control booth than I learned out of a textbook.

What was the first television variety special that you did and how did it come about?

After *The Smothers Brothers Comedy Hour*, I went to do *The Andy Williams Show* doing cue cards. The producer of *The Andy Williams Show* gave me an opportunity to direct my first television special. I'll try to make a long story very short: I went from cue cards to associate directing. But before I started in associate directing, I had the opportunity to direct three television specials. From *The Andy Williams Show*, I was offered an associate directing job on *The Sonny and Cher Comedy Hour*. The previous shows that I directed had been syndicated shows and *Sonny and Cher* was on the CBS network.

I decided to take a step back from directing to associate-directing, but it was really taking a step forward because I was moving into a network, prime-time, television series. I associate-directed that show for a couple of years, and then Fred Silverman, the head of CBS at the time, discovered a guy named Tony Orlando. Fred had been watching my work and hired me on *Tony Orlando and Dawn* to direct. We did four summer shows and the shows rated so well that Fred picked it up right away to go on the air immediately. That was my first real series as a director.

Is there anything in particular that you look for when choosing a project?

I look for a challenge. I like to do things where I know I can work hard and have fun. I do mostly variety shows and event specials. I've done just about everything except a full-length feature.

How long have you been directing **The Academy Awards?**

I've done it six times.

How important is it for a director to understand acting?

It depends on what kind of directing you're doing.

Let's say for **The Academy Awards.**

The Academy Awards is very difficult. You're dealing with movie stars as nominees and movie stars as presenters, who are not television performers normally, and they're nervous about being on a live show. They know that they're going to have to perform in a way that they usually don't perform—in front of a billion people. Actors and actresses are used to being able to do multiple takes of a scene. They're on a soundstage with a crew of a hundred people or so and that's it. Or sometimes less. All of a sudden they're on a live television show. They've been pushed out there by a stage manager, and they walk into a theater that has four thousand people sitting there and they're nervous. There are no second takes on a live show. So anyway, you have to be able to deal with that.

Is there a certain personality that makes a better type of director?

I think that, to be a good director, being secure and having the confidence in yourself and knowing that your instincts are right is most important. Being able to know how to communicate, not only for actors and actresses. When I do *The Academy Awards,* for example, I wear a headset and there's probably two hundred people on the other end of the headset listening to what I have to say. You've got to be able to communicate with cameramen and a stage manager, stage hands, grips, writers, art directors, and choreographers, as well as the actors. So communication is probably first on the list.

In the face of rejection, how do you maintain a sense of security?

You deal with it to the best of your ability. I've gone home sometimes after not getting a show that I really wanted, or having a very difficult day with an actor, and it just really gets you down. You just do the best you can and move on.

What is the most frustrating and then the most gratifying part of being a director?

I get frustrated when somebody doesn't deliver what they said they were going to deliver. I get frustrated when a writer delivers a script and it's not what we talked about. It's not my vision. When I'm actually doing the show, the things that are frustrating are the things that work beautifully on paper, and then you get into the theater and the set goes up and it doesn't look quite the same as it did on paper.

Gratifying. To me, everything is gratifying. I work as hard as I can work to make everything come out right. Sometimes you have to settle—you have to be willing to do that. I'm a perfectionist and I will try and get everything exactly the way that I want it. I've dealt with good talented people; nobody works for me, everybody works with me. I make everybody part of the family and I make everybody part of the project so that we all have the same goal.

JEFF MARGOLIS

On the shows that you've done, when you've produced and directed the same show, is that difficult?

It is difficult. It depends on the show. There are certain shows that I'll produce and direct on my own. But for most shows, I bring in a coproducer to work with me, because I need somebody to bounce off of. You get tunnel vision. And that's why I'm very aware of the people I work with. And most of the people come back show after show. They know me well enough to be able to say to me, "Absolutely great idea. But what do you think about this?" Which is what a coproducing partner does. Then at some point I have to take my producer's hat off and put on my director's. Since I like to give one hundred percent to everything that I do and you can't give one hundred percent doing two things at that same time. So that's why I like to bring somebody in.

At this stage of your career, what are your biggest challenges?

Every show that I do is a challenge. I look at each one as a new, different, exciting challenge. I don't ever take anything for granted and nothing ever becomes habitual with me. This year is my thirteenth year doing *The American Music Awards,* and each year I look at the show as a brand-new, first-time project. I do that with every show. Even when I was doing weekly series, I tried to look at each one of them as being special. So, what are my biggest challenges? The next show that I'm doing. Right now I'm trying to make some changes. I'm trying to get into some new areas, and I find that very challenging.

RUSSELL MULCAHY

Russell Mulcahy got his start directing music videos. "Hungry Like the Wolf," by Duran Duran, led to his first feature film. Some of the films he has directed include Highlander *and* Highlander II: The Quickening, Ricochet, The Real McCoy, *and an HBO Special entitled* Blue Ice. *His most recent film is* The Shadow, *starring Alec Baldwin.*

How did your career begin?

I always wanted to make movies. I picked up my first eight-millimeter camera when I was fourteen, which I still have. I used to cut film with scissors and hold it in my fingers with glue. I watched every movie I could and read any book I could find, especially those written by Russian filmmakers. I never went to film school; they rejected me.

So I became a film editor in Sydney, Australia, cutting the news for a local TV station. While I was there, I made a one-hour-long film which won an award at the film festival in Australia. Then I decided to do Video Clips (like MTV) in Australia because no one was making them over there. I did a video clip called *Hungry Like A Wolf* by Duran Duran. This led to my first feature film in Australia. I was then asked to direct *Razorback* on the back of that video. Next came *Highlander, Ricochet,* and other films, including *The Shadow.*

What skills should a director have?

From my point of view, not going to film school actually helped me with my skills, because I learned from my own mistakes. I think to be a good director you should go with your gut instincts. You also must be able to communicate with people you work with—writers, actors, etc. So communication is very important. You also have to have a keen visual sense.

RUSSELL MULCAHY

Is it important for a director to understand acting?

Absolutely. I used to be an actor onstage. I don't think that means you need to go to acting school, but you need to understand the craft. The actors breathe the life of the characters who will be on the screen. I am very open with actors. You have to have a very open relationship with them. There needs to be a trust on both sides. It's very important to know about every facet of filmmaking.

What is the director's relationship with the producer and screenwriter?

With the writer, the relationship is very strong up front, and very close. It's usually a three-way relationship—writer, producer and director. I personally will bring the writer to the shoot if something is not working. So the writer should always be on hand. The relationship with the producer starts before preproduction has even begun. We have already sat down and gone through production design, storyboard, script, casting, etc. He will suggest things, look at dailies...we will argue a lot. You need an open relationship with the producer—director/producer is like a marriage: short-term, but intense.

What do you look for when choosing a project?

Something I would want to see. I do like the genre of suspense and adventure, a form of fantasy like *Highlander.*

Have you ever tried to emulate anyone in your career?

Not on a day-to-day basis. My education was always doing my own thing. I admired European films. As a teenager, I was a big fan of Ingmar Bergman, Fellini, the early years of Ken Russell films—they had freedom in their work, which I liked. They broke rules; the camera crossed the line and it didn't matter—organized chaos, if you like.

How much rehearsal is necessary when preparing to shoot a film?

It really depends on the film. For *The Shadow,* we did two four-week rehearsal sessions before actually filming. There is some danger in overrehearsing. No actor wants to give it all away, because there is a chance that it will never come back.

RUSSELL MULCAHY

At this stage of your career, what are your greatest challenges?

In this country, I have never really hit the American mainstream. *Ricochet* did okay. *Highlander* did better in Europe. A few people saw it here.

Any further advice?

Have faith in yourself. There are no set rules how things happen. If you can, get a sixteen-millimeter camera, or whatever. Buy a roll of film each week and try to make a short film to show someone your talent—or the talent you think you have. It's something you must do yourself—it can't be handled for you. Make yourself different from what is out there. Go for it.

FRANK OZ

Frank Oz has been a motion picture director for the past ten years. Films to his credit include Little Shop of Horrors, Dirty Rotten Scoundrels, What About Bob? *and* House Sitter. *Frank has been with Jim Henson Productions for thirty years and is a vice president of the company. Other credits to his name include: coproducing (with David Lazar) and performing in* The Great Muppet Caper; *codirecting (with Jim Henson) and performing in* The Dark Crystal; *writing, directing, and performing in* The Muppets Take Manhattan; *and executive producing and performing in* The Muppet Christmas Carol. *Frank brought life to such muppet characters as Animal, Fozzie Bear, Sam Eagle, Miss Piggy, and, on* Sesame Street, *Cookie Monster, Grover, and Bert. and Yoda in* The Empire Strikes Back *and* Return of the Jedi.

Explain how your career began.

I was performing with *Muppets* and I would always make it a point to ask questions of the DP's [directors of photography], editors, and the crew. I tried to learn as much as possible without going to film school. Jim Henson, the creator of the *Muppets,* was interested in doing a film called *The Dark Crystal,* which he asked me to codirect. It was definitely Jim's film, but he thought I could help make it better. Jim then asked me to direct the third *Muppet* movie, which was the first film I actually directed on my own. Then David Geffen asked me to direct *Little Shop of Horrors,* which I did, and have continued to direct ever since.

Should an aspiring director attend film school?

I don't think it's essential. There have been many wonderful directors that have never attended film school.

FRANK OZ

Is it important for a director to understand acting?

There are a lot of directors that have never acted before and are great directors. I have taken a few years of acting, but whether that makes one a better director, I don't know.

What do you look for when choosing a project?

If when reading a script my heart pounds faster, and if I put it aside and it calls to me, then that is what I look for.

What is the director's role?

Number one, one must deliver the movie and keep perspective. You also have to get a lot of talented people to help do the film the way you see it.

What is the most frustrating and then the most gratifying part of being a director?

The most frustrating is being in a black room, looping for a month when it is sunny outside! It's also frustrating when you are on a film and you can't get things exactly right because of circumstances. It may be sunny outside and you need it to rain. Or you have one more scene to do and your actor is called off to California...things that you have no control over. The most gratifying is when you see something come alive—a moment, an emotion, a scene—that is the reason for directing.

What is your relationship to the producer and the screenwriter?

With the producer, there are different kinds of producers...one I have been in partnership with on several films is Bernie Williams, and my relationship with him is total trust. With regard to the screenwriter, I always love to have screenwriters in meetings and on the set as much as possible, as long as I'm the one who talks to the actors. Given that, I really enjoy having them on the set.

Do you emulate anyone in your directing?

No, not consciously. I certainly still have my standard favorites. Mostly the material tells me what to do when I direct a movie.

How much rehearsal is necessary to prepare for a film?

It depends on the actors and actresses and also on the schedule...it depends on a lot of things. I really like to have a couple of weeks of rehearsals before I start the movie. I first like to talk to the actors and screenwriters to see where the soft spots are. What I really like to do is explore the scene with the actors, do some preliminary blocking, and then leave things raw.

What is your relationship to the cinematographer?

Extremely close...similar to the screenwriter and producer. I rely on these people to help me get what I want. I also like to get their opinions. Whether I take their suggestions or not, I still have great respect for the cinematographer as I do for the crew members.

What further advice would you give an aspiring director?

The only advice I have is not to worry if a movie makes money or not...just have fun doing it. If it does not make money, at least you will know that you enjoyed doing it, and you hopefully will have learned and gotten some experience.

At this stage of your career, what are your greatest challenges?

Every time I do a movie, it's a challenge...it's starting fresh. When I look at good movies, I say to myself, "How did they do that? It's amazing!" I remember Orson Welles once said that he created out of innocence, and I think that's a good way to create. Doing any fresh movie is a challenge. I am looking forward to doing a drama, rather than a comedy. That would be a challenge for me at this time in my life.

PRODUCERS

LYNN BIGELOW

Producer Lynn Bigelow began her association with Jim Kouf in 1983, when she served as associate producer on two Greenwalt/Kouf pictures: Secret Admirer *and* Miracles. *Kouf and Bigelow (shown pictured together at left) became partners and, since 1985, have been associated with Walt Disney Studios. The first film they produced as a team was* Disorganized Crime. *Lynn recently completed executive production of the film* Kalifornia, *starring Brad Pitt and Juliette Lewis, for Propaganda Films.*

Would you explain how you got started in your career?

After college, I got a job as a secretary (they didn't have assistants in those days) at IFA, which was the agency that later became ICM [International Creative Management]. I then went into TV production at MTM [Mary Tyler Moore], which had just started up their hour-series division. I worked with a writer/producer for a year on a series and then went to Paramount and worked for Don Simpson, who at that time, was head of the studio. It was there I met Jim Kouf. I worked with Jim and his partner, David Greenwalt, on a couple of films as associate producer, and then Jim and I formed our own production company.

That's how I got into the business. Staying is another thing. I worked hard, listened constantly, and did everything I could to make the people I worked with trust me as much as they could. When people trust you, they give you more responsibility and, subsequently, more work. One of the ways to get in and be successful in this business is to try and work with the most talented people you can.

What is the role of the producer?

There are various different definitions of a producer, and every producer will probably tell you something different. I can just tell you what I do and why I get credit for it. The executive producer usually finds the script, sets it up at a studio or production company, and then proceeds to package the project. By packaging, I mean finding the director, actors, and various key produc-

LYNN BIGELOW

tion personnel. As executive producers, we also do what I think is the most important, and that is to get the script in shape: working with the writer, and eventually the director, to get the best possible script you can. The producer does about the same thing, just more of it. We like to develop a project from idea through script. And then the difference between the two producer credits is that the producer stays with the project through production and postproduction and release of the film.

The most important part of the equation of making a movie is the script—finding the best material. Obviously, making contacts in order to find these scripts is invaluable. You have to know the agents, solicit material...it takes a lot of time and patience.

What do you look for when choosing a project?

Very specifically, a good story.

Do you think attending film school is essential?

I don't think it's necessary. But then I would never discourage anyone from going to school. It's just not the route I took. The best thing to have as a producer, is good taste—and a lot of stamina. You need to know how to spot a good story, and then have the stamina to get beat up trying to get it made.

Is it important for the producer to be involved with casting?

It is very important. There are two things a producer needs to do, and this applies to casting as well as everything else in making a movie. One is to be involved and to fight for what you believe in. And the other (this is the hard one) is to know when to step back. It starts as the writer's movie. Then, once you have sold the project, it becomes the studio's movie. Then, when the director comes aboard, it's the director's movie. Hopefully, it will always be your vision, and that everyone is striving to make the same movie. But it's usually a constant battle—one that sometimes you win and sometimes you lose.

How important is it for the producer to be on the set?

Half and half—because if the producer is doing his or her job, then he or she shouldn't be on the set all the time. I think that the producers that want to be there all the time are: a.) not doing their job; or b.) probably want to be directors. For myself, I'm there because I'm dealing with the crew and cast, watching the director, and, quite frankly, because it's the only fun I have all day.

What are the most essential skills needed to become a good producer?

The ability to work with people...lots of different people, with lots of different egos and agendas. There's about nine different movies being made at one time. The art director is making his movie, et cetera, and you need to try to keep everyone in line and making the same movie. And, you have to make it work in the most efficient time and within a budget. It really is the ability to keep several balls in the air at one time.

What is the most frustrating and then the most gratifying part of being a producer?

There are several frustrating things...and these are not listed in order of frustration. One is having a good script and no one buys it. This happens all too often. Two is having a good movie then nobody goes to see it. Or three, at one point in the process you had a good movie, and somewhere along the line it gets screwed up by others involved.

The gratifying part is having none of these things happen. But if I had to fantasize about the most gratifying experience, it would be to make the movie you always wanted to make, have it come out good, people love it, and it's critically and monetarily successful.

With all the rejection in the business, how do you maintain a sense of security?

I don't get insecure about my job...I probably get cynical. You just gotta keep plugging along and do the best you can.

How do you decide who to cast in a film?

Sometimes when you read a script, someone might come to mind. Depending on what kind of film it is, what the budget is, and if it's a studio movie or not, you often go after the big star. It's also nice to get a great actor. Sometimes they're one and the same. Ultimately, you try to cast the best person and actor for the role.

TODD BLACK

For ten years, Todd worked as an independent producer with Joe Wizan. They made seventeen films together. He has produced such films as Split Decisions, Short Time, Becoming Collette, Stop! Or My Mom Will Shoot, *and most recently* Wrestling Ernest Hemingway. *Todd is now involved in a company with director Randa Haines.*

How did you begin your career?

I went to USC Drama School and studied under the John Houseman Julliard Program that he had brought with him to USC. I was an undergraduate theater-directing major even though they did not have a department. We created one. My senior year I was asked if I wanted to intern at a casting office at Twentieth Century Fox Studios. I said "yes" and was an intern on various television shows and feature films. I did that until I got out of college.

In May of 1982, Twentieth Century Fox hired me and I was a casting director from 1982–1984. I left because I felt casting directors did not have the power to make creative decisions that they once had in the '70s. I then opened up my own production company in the dining room of my home. I borrowed money from my family so I could start optioning material. I optioned a book by Lisa Birnbach called *The Official College Handbook*. I thought this would be a great idea for a movie. I then created a story and sold it to MGM.

One thing led to another, and eventually I ran out of money. I then met Joe Wizan who had been president of Twentieth Century Fox Studios, and after that had become an independent producer at Fox. He had a big overall deal and he hired me as an independent producer in his company. I then brought in six pieces of material that I had set up. So he said, "Anything you do, we'll produce together now." And he gave me a shot at it for one year. After the year, it worked, and eventually we became full partners. We were together for ten years and made seventeen films together.

TODD BLACK

What films have you produced?

Split Decisions, Short Time, Fire In The Sky and a film that my wife wrote called *Becoming Collette*. We also did others. Our most recent film is *Wrestling Ernest Hemingway*, with Robert Duvall and Richard Harris.

Do you still produce with Joe Wizan?

I am now involved in a company with the director Randa Haines. We met on *Wrestling Ernest Hemingway*. She was the director. Joe and I are on very good terms and will still produce films together.

Do you think film school is essential?

Not necessarily. I think a knowledge of film helps, but the most important thing you must have is the love of films.

Define the producer's role.

Every producer has a different job description. There are creative producers, financial producers, producers only looking to put talent together and walk away from it. There are producers that love finding the material. For myself, I think that I am the kind of producer who likes the overall scope. I love to work on it with the writer and with the director. Ultimately, I like to work with the director to make it a true collaboration. I am there from the beginning to the end—in the cutting room, scoring the music, mixing, marketing and advertising.

When is a director brought in to a project and how is he or she chosen?

I like to bring a director in as soon as I can...as soon as I have the script right. I don't care if the scripts are not set up. A lot of my movies were not set up at studios when I went to the director. I select the director based on the material that I think that he or she will respond to. Sometimes producers make mistakes because they will go to directors who have done similar things and that just doesn't work. I go to directors who haven't done anything similar to the film I'm submitting to them, but whose films have some related themes.

How important is it for a producer to get involved in casting?

It's key for me. I think when producers don't get involved their movies are usually miscast, and ultimately this can hurt the project. I do think that it's the directors choice, because he or she has to direct them. But I think it's important that there is another opinion in the room. The movies I have not been totally involved in were the movies I am not proud of. By the way, I don't think any producer sets out to make a bad movie, but it doesn't always turn out like you planned, for various reasons.

Is it important for a producer to have an agent?

No. I think it hurts you and limits you because other agencies don't want to send you scripts because they can't commission you. In the very beginning of my career, I had an agent who was very instrumental in helping with my deal with Joe Wizan. I think if someone feels that's what they need to break in, that's fine.

How do you get representation?

Material. You must have the right material with good strong characters. I will take anyone's phone call if I know that they have conviction about the material they have in their hands. I'm not interested in a story they have off the top of their head. But if they have a good script, good idea, good book, or good article, come to my office. I don't care where you come from.

Will you look at unsolicited material, that is, will you meet with anyone, even if they don't have an agent?

Even if you have no agent. I have found a lot of good material that way.

Are you involved in distribution and marketing?

I am very involved. Unfortunately when you don't own a piece of the picture, it's very hard to tell the distribution department at the studio exactly what you want them to do, but you can have some influence. I have gotten things I've wanted, but most of the people in distribution are smart and know what they are doing. It's ultimately all a crapshoot.

What do you look for when choosing a project?

Strong characters. Characters I know I can cast and actors are going to want to play. Producers and writers have to think about that: Is this going to be a piece that an actor is going to want to do? Is it different? Does it have a voice? That's basically what I look for.

TODD BLACK

Describe your relationship with the director.

Because I believe in collaboration, I feel every single producer needs a director, and every director needs a producer. Those who feel they don't are kidding themselves, because there are so many, and collaborating is so necessary. I think the film suffers when there is none. If you can collaborate together and not have it be about power, but have it be about what's on that screen and what people are watching...if you can collaborate this way, then the relationship between the producer and director really works.

Once the script is finished, how involved is the screenwriter?

I love having the writer involved. Steve Conrad, who wrote *Wrestling Ernest Hemingway,* was on the set every single day. The writer is the person that created it, and I feel writers are still not treated equally. I think it's a huge mistake. I think it's the biggest mistake Hollywood makes. I think if writers were treated as well as producers, directors, and actors, we would have better movies.

What is the most frustrating and then the most gratifying part of being a producer?

Everything and nothing! The most frustrating thing is getting people to believe what you believe, and not having them sway with the wind. Keeping your own conviction when you get in a place of power and not listening to twelve other chefs in the kitchen. Believing in your own recipe...that is definitely the most frustrating. The most gratifying is going to that theater and sitting down with a real audience and hearing them cry or laugh and seeing the writer's, director's, and actor's visions, along with your visions, up on the screen...that's very gratifying.

Is it important for the producer to be on the set?

For me, everyday. There have been movies that I haven't been on the set for one reason or another. I have learned that not being on the set was a mistake.

What essential skills does a producer need?

Learning to communicate with people. Being able to delegate and being secure with yourself, and making people feel good and important about what they do and who they are.

When faced with rejection, how did you maintain a sense of security?

(*Laughs.*) You have to keep a sense of humor. It's the movies—that's all it is. You have to be able to deal with rejection, because that's what the business is all about. So, I try to keep a positive attitude and a sense of humor.

At this stage of your career, what are your greatest challenges?

Getting the next movie made. I'm really doing what I want to be doing. I'm thirty-three years old and I'm making movies. I also want to be working with people that I like. I am to a point in my career where I can do that pretty much. I don't have to work with people I don't like, because it's too difficult making a movie. I don't want to say I've reached my goals, but I am very happy doing what I'm doing. I'm not looking for a big change. I want to keep making good films. I want to enjoy the benefits of being in this business. I think it's a real privilege. You get paid well and you get to lead a very interesting and diverse life. It's fun pulling up to the studio lot everyday and being in make-believe-land.

Any further advice?

Find a good piece of material. That's the way in. That's your calling card. I got in through material, not because anyone knew me. I used my instinct. Most people have much better instincts than they think, and they don't trust those instincts. Another thing I would like to add is: don't ever function out of fear.

MARTIN BREGMAN

Martin Bregman began his professional career in the motion picture business as one of the industry's leading business and personal managers. His client list included Al Pacino, Barbra Streisand, Faye Dunaway, Candice Bergen, Raquel Welch, Alan Alda, and many more, including some of today's top directors and writers. In 1973, he launched his career as a movie producer with the film Serpico, *starring Al Pacino. He has produced several successful films, such as* Dog Day Afternoon, The Seduction of Joe Tynan, The Four Seasons, *and* Scarface, *among many others. Additionally, Martin has broadened his activities to include cable and television production. He has recently finished the film* The Shadow, *starring Alec Baldwin.*

Would you briefly explain how you got started in your career?

I was an agent many years ago—a nightclub agent in the beginning—and then I became a manager. As a manager, you go out and find new young artists. Some of the young people I represented became very successful, such as Al Pacino, Faye Dunaway, Sandy Dennis, Alan Alda, and so on. I then expanded into other aspects of the business in terms of representing writers, directors, and an occasional producer. That is basically how I got started.

Can you define what the job of the producer entails?

I can only tell you what I do. Most everything I've done starts with me, whether it is a book, a magazine article, or an idea that came to me in the middle of the night. I will then go and find a writer who shares my vision. I function as his or her editor and as a backboard, which is my function throughout the entire film process. I become the conscience of the project.

When is the director brought in and how is he or she selected?

Once the first draft of the screenplay is completed, the director is selected by me, the same way you select an actor. There are some directors who are wonderful for a particular kind of project and not wonderful for others. I don't think David Lean could have directed *Airplane* or *Tootsie*. Casting a director is as important as selecting a writer or casting an actor.

So for you, getting involved in casting is essential?

Yes. I am not only involved...I share control of the casting with the director. We each have a veto.

How important is film school for a young person considering a career in producing?

It's important for no other reason than getting that young person familiar with the process of film-making.

What was the first film you ever produced?

Serpico.

What is the difference between producing for television and producing for the big screen?

There is a big difference. The kind of monies available to you in films is considerably more than there is in TV. If you have less monies available, you're going to hire writers, directors, and actors of a lesser category. But there is always the exception.

Describe the most essential skills.

Creative ability is the most important element in producing. The motion picture business is not a business. It's an art form.

What do you look for when choosing a project?

Whether or not it excites me. It's all subjective because it all starts with one's personal taste.

How involved are you in distribution and marketing?

Very involved. I am involved in every aspect of the making of the film, from inception to production to postproduction to marketing. Making a film is like designing a mosaic because you're working with tiny pieces and until it's all up there, you don't know what you've really created.

What is the most frustrating and then the most gratifying part of being a producer?

It's a series of frustrations. It takes a long time to get something to happen. The development process takes somewhere between two to three years. Dealing with studios, agents, actors, and directors is always difficult. All of it is frustrating. The process is gratifying for me when it's successful—not for monetary reasons—but when you get an audience to react, whether it's laughter, tears, or seeing them sit completely engrossed. That's exciting. When people come up to you and tell you they really love the films you've made, it makes it all worthwhile.

You've made some great films.

I've done some great films and some pretty lousy films. They all start out great.

What further advice could you give someone just getting started?

Knowledge and appreciation of material, and whatever writing experience you can get, will add to your abilities.

LARRY GERSHMAN

Larry Gershman, founder, Chairman, and Chief Executive Officer of World International Network (WIN), has a unique and diversified background in broadcasting. Larry has been involved in all aspects of the television industry, from producing to selling to station management to President of the MGM/UA Television Group, where he was responsible for all television production and worldwide distribution. Active in industry affairs, Larry has been either the chairman or the co-chairman of the International Emmy Awards for the past eleven years and has been elected a Life Fellow of the International Council of the National Academy of Television Arts and Sciences.

How did you get started in your career?

I started in television after I finished my Master's Degree at Penn State. I started out working for this very nice man, Ely Landau, who owned NTA, which then was a fairly important company in terms of distribution. Landau also owned WNTA Radio and Television in New York City.

Subsequently, I went on to become President of the MGM/UA Television Group. I was Landau's executive trainee with no salary for six months. I worked literally from seven in the morning until two in the morning for Ted Cott; he was the executive in charge of Broadcasting. I worked with him on television and finished up the day with a radio broadcast until one-thirty in the morning. It was great! I don't know anybody who had the breaks I had, because I got to learn to do everything. In those days, the unions were very cooperative, so I learned how to work a camera, how to deal with directors, and I also got a chance to write. It was truly thrilling.

What is the role of the producer?

Producers in television are different than producers in motion pictures. A producer in television basically controls the production. It's his project. Then you have to break down line producers and executive producers. Generally speaking, an executive producer is someone who has the project. They have acquired the rights or they have an idea for a project. Usually, it's a true story or book that they have optioned the rights to. That person would, normally, then go to a network and say, "How would you like to do a two-hour movie on x, y, z," etc. If it's a book or a true story, they would try to sell it and convince the network to develop the project.

LARRY GERSHMAN

Then, with the network, they hire the writer. Networks usually like to be involved in the process of developing the story. It's very rare that a network would entertain a finished script. There was one time recently when NBC was looking for a finished script, so a hole did open up. But normally they want to be involved and they would want to approve certain writers.

Networks also want to approve certain producers. They want to see the direction of the project. Basically, the first thing an executive producer does is to acquire the rights. Secondly, he or she sells it to a network and then starts developing the project to get it into position. When you get the final "go" you work with the network on casting and actually producing it. Then you get a line producer, director, casting, and then the final budget.

What skills are needed to be a producer?

That's hard to say because there are so many different personality traits that comprise a successful producer. For the most part, producers tend to be people who are outgoing and communicate well. Communication is an essential quality. They need the ability to handle pressure and to be able to distinguish good taste and what the public wants.

Is it important for a producer to have an agent? If so, how do you obtain one?

Most do have agents. I think it is important to have an agent for a couple of reasons. A powerful agency can very often work you into a package. Someone has a property and they may represent a writer and own the rights. If they can handle you as a package, as producer they can wheel you into a project.

If you have the right agent, they can also be a buffer with the network—you have someone who can argue all the problems. There's the chicken and the egg. Do you do your projects and then say, "Look what I have done?" Or do you go to an agent and say, "Hey, I'm a talented young guy—give me a break"? You stumble your way through. You are an assistant producer on a project; you finally get something going on your own and maybe an agent helps you sell yourself—maybe he doesn't. Or you have a tape to show of your project next time around.

There is no set plan. You've got to keep going and pushing one way or another to get there. If you are any good, you will eventually get there.

Is the producer involved in distribution and marketing of a film?

Rarely are producers involved, but it depends. Some producers have their hands in everything. That is not a criticism—it's just an observation. Personally, I believe that a good executive should let the distributor distribute and let the producer produce.

LARRY GERSHMAN

What do you look for when choosing a project?

From our point of view, I look for projects that will travel internationally. We are focused specifically on the international marketplace. It also must appeal to the U.S. marketplace in the first instance. I look for real live stories: best-sellers, like Jackie Collins, Sidney Sheldon—that kind of plot works—stories of women in jeopardy, mostly. We've done ninety percent of our projects based on true life incidents.

What are some of the television movies you've produced?

The *In the Line of Duty* series, *The FBI Murders*, *A Cop for the Killing*, *Street Wars*, etc. Also, *Last Best Year*, which had a brilliant script. John Erman directed that movie; Mary Tyler Moore and Bernadette Peters starred in it. It was a true story of a woman executive who was dying of leukemia and the relationship she formed with her psychiatrist. It was a wonderful story. We are, in fact, doing another one now called *A Message from Holly*, another true story.

What are the most frustrating and gratifying parts of being a producer?

The most frustrating is generally getting it all together. The timing: the network wants it, but there's one thing they don't like. So you solve that one problem and something else comes out of the blue. It's enormously frustrating. Getting the network to be on the same wavelength you are, to see the project as you see it and to support it and to go in the same direction is often difficult. It isn't just selling the project. It's important to make sure you both want to grow an apple tree. You get halfway done and find out one has planted a citrus tree while the other one is looking for apples. Then you have a problem later. It's really important to get on the same wavelength and know where you are going with it. The most rewarding part of producing is when it all comes together and you get that moment of gratification. You see it and you say, "I love it!" It's beautiful!

When is the director brought into a project?

The director is usually brought in early. Certain producers have certain directors they like to work with. There are directors who do certain kinds of projects. Producers often try to work with the same group—same line producer, same cameraman, same director—if they can. It doesn't always work that way. But if you are doing serious television, you try to use the same four directors in rotation.

At this stage of your career, what are your greatest challenges?

To keep it all going. It gets tougher every year. At the moment, I think one of the reasons it's tough is because of the economy. As a result, it just seems to be harder to get each project off the ground. So I'd have to say my greatest challenge is to keep it all together and growing.

DEAN HARGROVE

Dean Hargrove has long been recognized as one of television's most respected and successful writer/producers. His unique, creative talents have shaped many of the TV's most outstanding series for more than fifteen years. Mr. Hargrove is responsible for a long list of successful series, including Matlock, McCloud, Columbo, Jake and the Fatman, Father Dowling Mysteries, The Name of the Game, *and the continually, top-rated, ongoing series of two-hour* Perry Mason *television movies.*

Can you explain how you got started in your career?

I came to UCLA in 1961 as a graduate student in the film department. I was there for one semester, and during that time I started doing some writing. I got some of my work around town and got an agent. I then sold a script for a show called *Maverick.* Then I continued by writing for shows such as *The Bob Newhart Show,* which at the time was a half-hour, variety show on NBC. I also was the sole staff writer for *The Man from U.N.C.L.E.* and also wrote the pilot for *The Girl from U.N.C.L.E.*

Then in 1967, I came to Universal Studios to work on *It Takes a Thief.* I was brought in to become the associate producer on the show for the first thirteen episodes. Then the studio moved me over to another show, *The Name of the Game,* which was a rotating series starring Gene Barry, Robert Stack, and Tony Franciosa. I became the writer/producer on the Gene Barry episodes. I stayed with that show for three years.

I then wrote the second pilot for *Columbo,* a two-hour movie called *Ransom for a Dead Man* and produced and executive-produced the series for three years. Finally, after ten years, I left Universal and went to Viacom. Fred Silverman had acquired the rights to *Perry Mason.* I partnered with him and wrote the first two-hour movie, *Perry Mason Returns,* in 1985. It was a very big success commercially. We then did the second movie, which did even better. Then we went into business doing these movies on a regular basis. I developed the "Matlock" character for

DEAN HARGROVE

Andy Griffith and Joel Steiger, and I developed *Jake and the Fat Man,* with William Conrad and Joe Penny. At the moment we are doing a series of TV movies with Dick Van Dyke. So I would have to say starting out as a writer led to my career as a producer.

Can you define the role of the television producer?

My experience is limited to two-hour movies and series. I have been away from the two-hour movies for a while now. So I can tell you what a television producer does for a series. In terms of series television, the producer is the one who controls the show. He hires the directors and delivers the script. I became a producer because I had the experience in delivering scripts. Now we have a writing staff, and sometimes we use freelance writers. The producer's job is to focus on the writing—that's the most important job.

How important is it for you to get involved in casting?

It is very important. All of these aspects cannot work if it is not cast properly. Many times, if you are developing a series and the casting goes wrong, it can be a very serious problem in the development process. Quite often, people are looking for the same kind of actor, and that is not always possible. So many times compromises are made, and that can be very damaging because you get the wrong casting. Our experience is to try and start with the performer and develop the series for him or her. From my point of view, casting is critical.

What is your opinion of film schools?

I think it is a good idea, but I don't think it is essential. I think it gives you a clear point of view, and if you are going to be a writer/producer, it gives you a strong knowledge of film history.

What is the most frustrating and then the most gratifying part of being a producer?

The most frustrating part is when everything goes wrong on a series. And when one thing goes wrong, it will go wrong all the way, starting with the script to the casting of the show. The most gratifying is naturally when everything turns out well.

Can you recommend any good books or courses one can take?

Since I started out as a writer, I would tell someone to get involved in writing seminars or writing courses offered by UCLA extension. In regard to books, two I would recommend are: *The Art of Dramatic Writing* and *Screenplay.*

At this stage of your career, what are your biggest challenges?

The greatest challenge for me is to improve my abilities and not get repetitive. When you do television work, it requires you to come up to bat often, so you have to rely on your strengths. That can be limiting.

In the face of rejection, how did you maintain a sense of security?

When I began in 1961, there was a lot more television than there is now. There were ten more hours of prime time. A series wasn't twenty-two episodes, it was thirty-six to thirty-nine episodes. If you had any facility at all, you were going to work. It wasn't difficult for me to get in the business at that time. I was twenty-two years old and making a living at it. Rejection was not a serious problem for me. I think people starting today have a much more difficult time. The marketplace is much more narrow.

When is a director brought in, and how is he or she selected?

They are selected based on previous work. Either you have seen their work, or an agent submits their work. Then I usually meet them to see what their personality is like and if they will fit into the needs of the show. Then the director is brought in on the first day of preparation. The director gets one day of preparation for each day they shoot.

What further advice can you give to a person wanting to pursue a career as a producer?

Perseverance is the most important trait you can develop. Particularly today, because there are a lot of talented people. Also, film school is useful for building aesthetics and a strong point of view in what you are doing. So stay strong and confident, and don't give up.

JONATHAN KRANE

A former tax lawyer and Yale graduate, Jonathan Krane now produces feature films. He has produced over twenty-five features, including Blind Date, The Chocolate War, Micki and Maude, A Fine Mess, The Man Who Loved Women, *and—one of the most profitable films in Tri-Star history—*Look Who's Talking Now.

Explain how your career began.

I was a tax lawyer in a large law firm doing international film financing deals. I represented some foreign directors and actors. Independent producing at that time was fairly simple because there were tax shelters and a lot of money available. Peter Hoffman, who was president of Carolco Pictures, worked on those deals with me at the law firm. We were both from Yale Law School.

I then met my wife, actress Sally Kellerman, whom I attended parties with and found her friends to be much more interesting than my lawyer friends. So, I decided to change professions. And at the time, I had been a lawyer for five years and coming out of Yale University, I was making a good salary.

But I needed a change. So I approached Blake Edwards, whom I knew. He was a fiercely independent producer and did not like the studio system and had a complete foreign lifestyle, being a resident of Switzerland. So what I did was to propose to him a new idea of starting a company by using all these different techniques for independent producing, so that he could make movies without using the studio system. So, I basically bootstrapped myself as a producer, which was very difficult because you have to find an angle and a player and put them together.

Which films have you produced?

Twenty-six features: *The Trail of the Pink Panther, Curse of the Pink Panther, The Man Who Loved Women, Micki and Maude, A Fine Mess, That's Life!, Blind Date, You Can't Hurry Love, Slipping Into Darkness, The Chocolate War, Bud The Chud, The Experts, Look Who's Talking, Getting It Right, Catch Me If You Can, Chains Of Gold, Boris and Natasha, Fatal Charm, Limit Up, Breaking*

219

JONATHAN KRANE

The Rules, Without You I'm Nothing, Convicts, Cold Heaven, Look Who's Talking Too, Look Who's Talking Now, and *Love Is A Gun.*

Describe the role of the producer.

Producing a film has five steps: the first is coming up with an idea; step two is developing a script; three, packaging, which is getting the director and actor involved; four, financing; and five, the last step, is physical production. The basic emotion that drives this business is fear, which leads to a follower mentality. A producer must be fearless so others will jump on his bandwagon.

Another principle is credibility. You become credible as a producer when you achieve the five steps by yourself. To the extent you overcome obstacles, you create credibility for yourself. Another dynamic is clout. Clout comes with success in scaling the five steps. Also, building talent relationships is very important in creating clout. When I was CEO of Blake Edwards Entertainment, I started a management company to get access to talent. It worked well for me. When I took MCEG public, I had fifty clients, all with scripts they were passionate about. To be a successful producer, talent and persistence both play major roles.

Do you still manage?

I only manage one person, John Travolta.

Do you work closely with the casting director?

Not for the lead roles. To cast those is part of packaging and occurs prior to pre-production. I pursue talent who work on a creative and business level. Once the movie is "greenlighted," I bring in a casting director to help find fresh faces for the smaller parts.

Is being on the set essential?

If you've done your job right as a producer, you are really only a troubleshooter during principle photography. You are very involved with preproduction and postproduction, but do not have to be on the set. I teach a class at UCLA on how to become a producer. I tell my class that the good producer is the only guy who could die during a film and nobody would notice.

What is your opinion of film schools?

Film school cannot prepare you to be a producer. It might help if you want to be a director. I don't think there are any set rules. No school you could go to could teach you how to convince a studio to make you a producer. Producers are people who come in with packages. I think working for a producer might help. For myself, I give everyone who works for me an opportunity to learn.

What is your opinion of law or business school as preparation for a producer?

I always advise people not to go to law school...it is incredibly difficult to move from lawyer to being a producer, because this town dislikes lawyers. I don't think lawyers wanting be producers, in general, are taken seriously, but on occasion, it does happen. If you go to business school and get a degree, what you are told, if you start interviewing, is to get into business affairs. But business affairs is a dead end if you want to be a producer. I am one of the few guys I know that has done both things.

What is the most frustrating and the most gratifying part of being a producer?

The most frustrating is getting the movie made. Getting the right material and getting it to the right talent—and getting the studio to like it—can be a very frustrating process. The most gratifying is if you have optioned a script and a studio buys it, because that means you and some studio executive are on the same wavelength creatively. Also gratifying is making successful movies. I made a film, *Look Who's Talking Now,* which was the most profitable film in Tri-Star history. That was very rewarding. Teaching my classes at UCLA extension has been the most rewarding. Sometimes it's been more gratifying than making pictures.

What do you look for when choosing a project?

Something I feel passionate about, something with heart. Every project I have has a star director, which I think helps the film.

What essential skills does a producer need?

You need to be thick-skinned with a short memory. You have to be able to live with rejection. You need talent and perseverance. If you don't have these skills, being a producer would be wrong. You must be able to figure out every obstacle, in front of you.

Any further advice?

I tell my classes something which pertains to every aspect of Hollywood: Hollywood is a state of nature. What that means is that there are no rules. You can't get a degree in producing. You can't go to school and come out and say, "Now I have the job at the studio." You become a producer by becoming a producer. Another way one could get in is by writing a brilliant script, [and] everybody finds out about it. That doesn't happen very often...maybe once a year, but it does happen.

WILLIAM LINK

William Link, a producer and a writer, is the creator (along with the late Richard Levinson) of the hit TV show Columbo. *From there, he has gone on to do various other TV projects, including* The Execution of Pvt. Slovik, The Boys, *and* That Certain Summer. *Currently, he is the executive producer of* The Bill Cosby Mysteries.

Would you briefly explain how you got started in your career?

I started my career with my partner, Richard Levinson (who is now deceased), whom I worked with for several decades. We both attended the Wharton School of Business, and while there, we sold short stories to *Playboy* and various mystery magazines. We also wrote the university musicals and we spec'ed television scripts. We decided not to go into a business career. (It was so much more fun in show business, even on that level.) We decided to go to Hollywood. That is where all the television shows had gone. We went into [a] contract with Four Star Television. (They were the biggest television producers on the planet.) Dick Powell was one of the owners of Four Star. It was an incredible time, and we got our feet wet there. We learned production. We were story editors under contract.

What was the first thing you wrote that was recognized?

We wrote a mystery-drama. It was about a psychiatrist committing the perfect murder, and into his life came a shambling, bumbling policeman by the name of Columbo. And that was really the beginning of us as writers. It became a big hit.

Do you think film school is necessary for a person considering a career as a writer today?

From a writer's point of view, I don't think you can teach writing. A screenwriter you can teach rudimentary things, like writing character, but I don't think you can learn structure—it's a God-given gift. Therefore, I think if you want to hedge your bets out here as a writer or producer (I'm speaking of these two fields because that's what I do), I think you can hedge your bets by maybe getting a degree in something else you can always fall back on, because this is an incredibly competitive business. Everybody wants to do it, either for glamour or the money. There's actually very little glamour. There is money, but the majority of people don't make big money in this field. Most people starting out don't know that. Maybe it's better that they don't because it doesn't cut into or limit their ambition. It's best to think you're going to have the world on a string, and just work, work, work!

Since writing is such a competitive field, how did you maintain a sense of security when faced with rejection?

Well, I was lucky because I had a partner. We were also best friends. Because the resistance factor out here is so strong, it's better two against the world than one. The one good thing about writing is you are not rejected personally. You're not targeted as much as an actor. So I would have to say it was not as difficult because I had someone to reinforce me, which is very good psychologically.

Where do you derive your ideas from?

Anywhere. A person might tell me something, a story. I do a lot of reading. You don't steal, but I might be reading a book and I think the author's going to go in a certain direction in a novel and they don't, and instantly I'll see a whole other way to go. Newspapers. I read three newspapers a day. I think as a writer you've got to have tremendous input.

When you write, how do your characters evolve?

The most important part of the process is the germination period. When I've got the concept, which to me is the most important element, then I find the characters. And as I work them out, I begin to see them.

What is your opinion on letting other people read your scripts before they're finished?

Never. And I would say that as a general rule for writers. Unless you have a real cheering section, or a very sympathetic wife or girlfriend who loves everything that you do, it can really undercut your enthusiasm. You've got to keep yourself revved up and enthusiastic, and you've got to be your own cheerleader. You don't want anyone interrupting that process.

Have you ever thought about directing any of the scripts you've written?

No. I'm probably the only writer in town that can make that statement. You'll never find me directing, because I know my weaknesses. And I don't play to my weaknesses. I would not be a good director.

Since you also produce, could you briefly define the job of the producer?

You find the material and the writer (if you don't write it yourself.) You develop the screenplay, which I think is the most crucial. You've got to work off a good script. The writer is the only person who starts with a blank page. Every other person is a reactive artist. They react to something that is given to them, namely the screenplay. But a producer can shape and mold that story to begin with. Then you've got to get the financing, a good director whom you're compatible with, whom you respect. Then, casting, which is a crucial part of the process. Sometimes, the writer just stays in the room, creates his baby, then hands his baby over. I can't recommend that. If you create your child, you better take care of that child by being involved in the process, i.e., be a producer.

How does someone find a producer who will read unrepresented material?

I would try any hit show. Most television shows now have in-staff producers and writers. But occasionally you will find people who will read outside scripts. It's done. It happens. You have to ferret them out, because they can't find enough good material.

What type of skills would someone need to be a successful producer?

I think as a producer it helps to be a great bullshit-artist, because you're selling all the time. I also think being a great politician. Steven Spielberg, who directed the first on-the-air *Columbo,* was a wonderful politician, and I use the word politician in a good way. He had a wonderful method of handling people and working with the crew. At twenty-one years old, you could tell that he was going to go very, very far. And I think you need that. You've got to be a social animal. That's why a lot of writers don't produce—they're reclusive people. That's a major asset. If you're good with people, you can handle people.

What suggestions can you give with regard to obtaining representation?

That's very, very difficult. Several new writers a week want to know how to get into the business. As a writer, you've got to get your material to a good agent. And the bad thing is, agents won't look at your material unless you have a credit. What do you do if you don't have a credit? It's a catch-22 situation. So what I suggest is to knock on doors and try to get a name for yourself in television first. There is good money. You can pay your bills, enjoy yourself, and learn your craft!

What further advice would you give someone getting started in a career as a writer?

You've got to write, write, write. And you've got to speculate. That phone is not just going to ring— you must spec scripts. If it's a great story, I'll read your script, but you've got to sit down and write it. Writers write. You have to learn how to go into a room of strangers with power and sell them on a story that they've never heard before. That's a real gift. Get good at telling your stories. But keep working, all the time, seven days a week. Discipline. You've got to get a regimen of writing.

GEORGE LITTO

A professional Jazz saxophonist and a former agent, George Litto has gone on to produce many fine films. George's credits as a producer include such films as Dressed To Kill, Blow Out, Obsession, *and* Kansas.

How did you begin your career?

I was always an avid movie buff. I would see several movies a week. My introduction to the entertainment industry was as a musician. I became a professional jazz saxophonist. I was then introduced to the William Morris Agency in New York through a family friend. I wanted to pursue music, but my first position—after working in the mail room—was in theater, which I knew nothing about. I learned quickly, however.

What is the producer's job? Is the producer involved in casting?

A producer finds a good story, then a good writer. If the studio likes the script, then a director is brought into the project and actors are cast.

A producer is also very involved in casting. Actually, a good producer should be involved in everything—from creativity and organization, to financing and distribution. To me, the true definition of a producer is about five or six different jobs.

What is your opinion of film schools?

Any kind of formal education is important. As far as film schools go, I definitely think they could be a great help.

What do you look for when choosing a project?

I am in this business to do what I like to do. I like to be involved in films with which I feel some connection. I have a broad spectrum of taste. I'll work with something that will involve me and, hopefully, the audience. The audience will tell us if it's a good film by the amount of tickets they buy.

GEORGE LITTO

What skills does one need to be a producer?

You have to be able to initiate, or there is no film. You have to be somewhat aggressive and able to get things going.

What are the most frustrating and most gratifying parts of being a producer?

The most frustrating is having the film not work out, even with all the good help you get from others. Sometimes, it just doesn't work out the way it was planned. The most gratifying thing is when it works and the film has a continuing value.

Did your formal education have any bearing on your career?

Yes. I was always interested in the arts and in business. One of the reasons I became an agent was to work with creative people. Then, becoming a producer was to learn about business in a creative arena.

How do you maintain a sense of security when faced with rejection?

You have to have regard for yourself. You have to have regard for what you do and what you contribute. You need a sense of security that comes from your own ability. Then, you should incorporate that into your work. If you are in this business, you are going to have many difficult times, so keeping peace within yourself will help you through.

What suggestions do you have for obtaining representation?

Learn the business and represent yourself. You must always represent yourself even when you have a representative. When you really know what you want, then direct your agent and let him know what you really want from your career. You'll then be helping the agent as well as yourself.

What advice would you offer someone who wants to pursue a career in the entertainment industry?

You should only get into this business for the love of it. You have to like the work and the involvement with everyone. This business is about the thrill of creation. Don't be in it for the glamour or money. If you get into the entertainment industry for the wrong reasons, you will find it too frustrating, and it will make you a very unhappy person.

At this stage of your career, what are your greatest challenges?

Staying happy and having another successful film. It's a challenge to keep good films coming.

DAVID PERMUT

David Permut is a producer involved in all phases of the films he produces. Some of the films that he has produced include Dragnet, Blind Date, Three of Hearts, Captain Ron, 29th Street, Consenting Adults, *and* The Marrying Man.

Would you explain how your career began?

I was a variety agent. It was a great stepping stone. The contacts I made were very beneficial. Relationships are what the business is about.

Explain how education and/or training might have had a bearing on what you do today.

I made a number of eight-millimeter films. I made a Yiddish version of *Gone With the Wind* called "Gone With the Vind." My Aunt Ida played Scarlet and I was Rhett Butler. Then I made a movie with my housekeeper which was her fantasy...to have a role reversal with my mother. So my mother became the maid and the maid became my mother. I then took my films to the California Institute of the Arts. A professor there looked at them and said, "Son, did you ever think of being a producer?" Fortunately, he gave me good advice. Education is always important, whether it's by way of film school or going out and being a gofer on a movie set. The more you know, the better off you are.

Can you define the role of a producer?

It all starts with an idea. Sometimes the ideas don't come from me. I listen to writers. I read scripts, books, and newspapers. Once you have the idea, the producer will work with the writer to cultivate the project. Then I will bring all the packaging together: casting, directors, cinematographer—everything...being involved in all phases. Then, of course, the producer oversees day-to-day production and budget.

DAVID PERMUT

What is the most gratifying part of being a producer?

The most gratifying is cashing the checks!

What is the most frustrating part of being a producer?

The most frustrating is when the checks bounce! It's also frustrating when you want to achieve things much faster than they happen. The wheels don't turn that fast, and you are looking for commitments with millions of dollars to make movies. But the bottom line of it is, if you believe in it and you have the conviction to stay with it, eventually it gets made.

What do you look for when choosing a project?

Personal taste. You look at market trends. There are certain studios looking for specific projects for actors that they have deals with which occasionally enters into the equation.

Is it important for the producer to be involved in casting?

It is very important. It usually can mean the difference in making a picture or breaking it, and it doesn't necessarily have to mean star quality. You need good, confident actors. If you look at some of the star-driven films that have been box-office bombs, they are quite numerous. If you look at other pictures, like *Home Alone,* that [film] virtually had everything bringing all the packaging together: casting, directors, cinematographer, costumer—everything...being involved in all phases.

What is the difference between television and film, from a producer's point of view?

Often you read something in the newspaper, something that is timely, issue-oriented—something that is important. These are made into issue-oriented TV movies. Sometimes you can get a TV movie made a lot quicker than a feature film. I have worked on features for ten years. *Three of Hearts* I had worked on for six years. In the television business, once you get the "go," you are off to the races. You make the movie and it happens very quickly. The shooting schedule is a third of what it is on most features...twenty-some odd days to shoot your movie in. Your budget restrictions are a factor, and also, it's television-sponsored by corporations, so you have to conform to those restrictions. There have been a lot of terrific movies made for television.

How involved is the producer in the distribution and marketing of a project?

You need to be involved in everything. If you put your heart and soul into a movie, you want to know how the campaign is going to go. You want to be involved with the cutting of the trailer, the music, the selling and marketing of the film. To try and insure the success of all the films that I have been involved in, I take as active a role as I can, in that aspect of it. Jeff Katzenberg [Chairman of Walt Disney Studios] always says filmmaking is about compromise. And it is true. I think you never want to sacrifice the integrity of what you are doing, or your beliefs, but you have to keep punching away.

What are the most essential skills needed to be a producer?

You have to have a good instinct for stories, because it all starts there. You have to have a great script, then you have a foundation. If you have a bad script, then it doesn't matter who is producing, starring in, or directing or anything else. People have to be interested in the story, and that, to me, is one of the most important things. You have to be able to stand rejection...you need to hang in there. If you believe in anything, and if you want something bad enough, then you will get it! When you come to this town, you make it your business to know people: you read the trade papers; you see who is running what studio. Perseverance is an essential skill.

Is it essential that the producer be on the film set?

It is very important. I think the difficulty I had this past year was shooting four films at the same time. I was on the set as much as I could be with these films, but they were being done in all different parts of the country. I do, however, think a producer should do his best to be on the set as much as possible.

How do you choose your crew for a film?

It is a collaborative effort. It's not just one person who makes the decision. Filmmaking is about collaboration, and it's the director, the studio, financing, and, for myself, it's getting in a room and talking about who is best suited for the film. It also relates to other aspects of the film: who's going to be the wardrobe person, who's going to be the cinematographer...those decisions are all collaborative.

At this stage of your career, what are your greatest challenges?

My challenges have been consistent since I have been producing. I try to make films that affect people emotionally. To try and achieve financial and creative success is always the goal with any film.

SCOTT STERNBERG

Emmy Award-winning television producer Scott Sternberg and his Scott Sternberg Productions is presently partnered with Tony Danza's Katie Face Productions at Sony Studios. He is also serving as the Executive Producer of the upcoming MCA/Universal-distributed talk show, The Suzanne Somers Show. Scott and Tony produced the special entitled The Road to Hollywood, *featuring Arnold Schwarzenegger, Sharon Stone, and Eddie Murphy, for NBC, and the celebrity special* Before They Were Stars, *for ABC. Scott has also produced such game shows as* Hollywood Squares, Love Connection, The Dating Game, *and many others. As a producer/ director, his credits include PBS's* A Special With George Carlin *and* A Special With David Wolper, *which won an Emmy for Best Informational Special.*

How did your career begin?

After college, I got a job as a page at NBC. While working as a page, I got a job on a game show called *The Wizard of Odds.* Before I got that job, I had other jobs. I was a runner for Dick Clark Productions, and then I worked for Marty Pasetta as a coordinator for *The Wizard of Odds,* which was Alex Trebek's first show in the United States. As a coordinator, I was responsible for getting all the material from the writers, and making sure all the visuals were on the screen. I did a little bit of everything; it was a good learning experience, and it helped my career get started.

Define the role of the television producer.

The responsible person making sure that the vision of the show is in fact delivered. Putting together the right team of people to deliver that vision. Being responsible for managing the creative people who are involved in the day-to-day operation of a television show. As an executive producer (which I do more now), I am involved in creating and putting together the idea, going out and selling the show, and packaging the show and putting it on the air.

SCOTT STERNBERG

How important is it for you to get involved in casting?

It's very important because the vision has a lot to do with the talent that is on the screen, so you want to make sure you cast the right people.

What is your opinion of film schools?

I think they are very important because you get hands-on experience. You get to interact with different people; you get to understand how to communicate with other people. You have a chance to use it as a laboratory: to develop your craft and experience and see if it's film you are interested in, or television, or radio—what areas you are strong in, whether it's the creative side, the technical side, or the promoting side. So I think they can be very helpful, yet there is nothing like hands-on experience.

In the face of rejection, how do you maintain a sense of security?

I am never secure! I think you either do well on a job or you don't do well on a job. I've been fired and hired, so rejection is there all the time. It's a risky business, but I always knew I would survive.

Can you recommend any available books or courses?

UCLA Extension courses in Southern California are very good, because they have special guests that come into the classes from different entertainment fields, which is very helpful. Starting this fall, I am going to be teaching classes at San Marino High School on how to put together a television show.

How involved are you in the distribution and marketing of your shows?

When I was Executive V.P. at Guber/Peters, I was very involved in the distribution process (which was working with the sales people, visiting and selling to the stations), and even now, when I do projects, I feel I can be very helpful because of my experience with distribution and marketing.

When is a director brought in, and how is he or she selected?

The director comes in at the beginning of the project, after it has been sold and is ready for production. The director has a lot of input in terms of the look of the set, the lighting, and the technical aspect, so you want the director as soon as possible. The actual process of finding someone is trying to find someone who fits the format—somebody who possibly has done the format before.

Credentials also make a difference on certain projects. Sometimes I just go with my gut feeling—the energy, spirit and knowing that person can do the job.

What do you look for when choosing a project?

I always look for things that are different, unique, and that have an edge...something I know I can throw myself into and give a hundred and fifty percent.

Is it important for a producer to have an agent?

I think it is. An agent can get the producers to the places they need to go: he is looking out for what's going on, and an agent has good contacts. And, it's the way the business works today.

Any further advice?

Don't do it! But if you must do it, then do it right. Don't stop, be passionate about what you want to do, and never get to a place where you say, "If only I had tried..." Get all the "ifs" out of your system and don't give up!

STEVE TISCH

Steve produced his first feature film, Outlaw Blues, *starring Peter Fonda and Susan St. James, in 1977. His other credits include such films as* Risky Business, Bad Influence, Forrest Gump, *starring Tom Hanks, and most recently,* Corrina, Corrina, *starring Whoopi Goldberg and Ray Liotta. In addition, he also produced the highly acclaimed television movie,* The Burning Bed, *and two HBO Movies,* Judgment *and* Afterburn.

Explain how you began your career.

I went to school in Boston in the late '60s and while in school, I was able to get jobs working on films being shot in New York. During the summer of 1971, I was the assistant to Otto Preminger on *Such Good Friends.* I worked as an assistant to Peter Guber, who was then head of production at Columbia Pictures in Los Angeles. I worked for Peter for almost four-and-a-half to five years, and then, when he became vice president, I was able to get involved in all facets of production—script development, choosing directors, writers, and so on. It was like going to graduate school. It was a wonderful experience. In 1976, I decided it was time to go out on my own and become a producer...to really do it for myself. By taking risks, I started my own company, and it worked out well.

What was the first film you produced?

A feature called *Outlaw Blues,* starring Peter Fonda and Susan St. James. It was shot in Austin, Texas, and was a modern-day western with music. The movie cost under two million dollars, and I was right there everyday producing my first film in 1977.

Describe the job of the producer.

I think every producer defines what he or she does differently. Different producers bring a totally different agenda, personality, and behavior to the job. I am a producer who really is out there on a day-to-day basis. I try to identify material, read scripts, work with writers. I am fortunate

STEVE TISCH

because I have had careers as a producer in features and television. I have produced about fifteen movies for television, three or four series, and about fourteen features. I am involved from day one.

I don't think there are many producers who really have a total, hands-on approach like I do. I think there are fewer of us everyday. I am very proud of my career. My track record is good, and my relationships with actors, writers, and directors is extremely good. To have a good reputation helps in this business.

What do you look for when choosing a project?

As a producer, I ask myself, "Do I want to physically commit the time to make this movie? Would I want to see this movie?" As a person interested in trying to make this world a little better place, I ask myself, "Do I care about this movie?" Many of my movies have been made for television and were controversial...movies about real people in unfortunate situations.

I did a movie for television, *The Burning Bed,* and a movie for HBO called *Judgment,* about a Catholic priest who molested and sexually abused altar boys. I did another HBO movie called *Afterburn.* The issues I deal with are very uncomfortable, very controversial, and not always embraced by the majority. I think that movies can educate people and help them see things differently in their own lives—that's the kind of criteria that I apply when I make a movie. The older I get, the more choosy and picky I become, and I want to become *more* selective.

How important is it for the director to get involved in casting?

It is critical. Casting was very important in many of the movies that I have done. I feel that there is a lot of talent in this country, and I don't limit my casting to Los Angeles. I go to New York, Chicago, Dallas, and Montreal to look for actors, especially young actors. Casting can make the difference between a movie and a very successful movie. When I produced *Risky Business,* I don't remember the exact numbers of actors we saw across the country. The one agreement that the director, my partner and I had was that we were going to be very professional, precise, and very honest, until we found the right guy, which was Tom Cruise. Many studios and producers can become lazy when a major actor expresses an interest in a project, even though they may be wrong for the part. To be able to say "yes," you also have to be able to say "no."

When do you bring a director into a project and how are they selected?

Most of the time, I bring in the director myself. The way I work is to bring in a director early in the process. It's a little different with television. Once the feature starts, the director becomes the head of the company and the producer has to step back a little, because features are a director's medium. In television, the director is more like a junior partner to the producer, because television is more a producer's medium. I have always attempted to make the director in both mediums my partner. I try to go out of my way to support the director, but I try not to impose my vision too strongly as to what the movie should be, but to really work as a partner. So far, it has worked out very well.

Is it important to attend film school?

Film school can be a great forum to which people can learn and explore and meet other people...to be able to take chances and risks...a safe place to succeed or fail. You can definitely learn the technique and be forced to write and create. I have seen a lot of student films, and eighty percent are very predictable and twenty percent show talent, vision, originality, and sometimes growth.

On the other hand, I think that film school can also be very misleading. People that come out of film school sometimes are under the impression that producers, agents, and studio executives are going to literally knock on their door that night holding out scripts and contracts—it doesn't work that way. It's like anything else. If you want to get a sense of reality, it can be very important. However, it is often too painful. As we all know, the environment of school is an unreal sanctuary, and until you get out in the real world and realize that no one will take care of you, it's a tough racket. But talent, I honestly believe, will be identified. I encourage people to go to film school and work on low-budget films for the experience, and I also encourage people to try and not be disappointed. But don't give up, because if you really have a dream, this is one of the few businesses where you can make it come true.

What are the most essential skills one needs to be a producer?

You need to be thick-skinned. You have to be really prepared for rejection. Be a good salesman and a fairly good politician. Have some taste. Identify commercial ideas and be patient. You have to be a mother, father, babysitter, husband, and wife, and really understand that you are in a business that you cannot predict what will happen next. Most importantly, you have to act quickly and make good, sound decisions.

What is the most frustrating and then the most gratifying part of being a producer?

Very simple: getting the movie made is extremely gratifying. The most frustrating is that movies are getting made for the wrong reasons...there is a lot of fear running in the business right now. The

STEVE TISCH

business is also extremely competitive. For instance, many studio executives don't have the passion for what they're doing, and that can be very frustrating. Another gratifying aspect is to have a vision, a passion, and a desire to work with people who care as much as I do.

What further advice would you give an aspiring producer?

You have to love the business. You can't get disappointed or disillusioned. Don't let your parents talk you out of it. And if you really think you have talent, you have to fight it out, because it's a war everyday. You have to be good because it's a tough business. There are not many of us who get to play everyday. If you think you are good, go for it! Don't be afraid of the competition.

At this stage of your career, what are your greatest challenges?

I want to focus more on quality and not quantity. I do want to make movies that people care about and that may affect their lives and change the way they think about things. I want to keep making controversial films and television movies—they have proven to be a great area for me.

JOE WIZAN

Joe Wizan has produced many fine films. His very first film was Jeremiah Johnson, *starring Robert Redford. His credits include* And Justice for All, Tough Guys, Split Decisions, Fire in the Sky, *and most recently,* Wrestling Ernest Hemingway.

How did your career begin?

I went to the William Morris Agency as a trainee in 1958, then later I became an agent. I left William Morris in 1967, and then went to London to form a branch office. One of my partners was Alan Ladd, Jr. We were in business for seventeen months. I then went to CMA, another agency, for about a year and decided to step forward and produce.

Define the producer's role.

The single most important thing is trying to identify good material. The job of the producer is to get material that will attract elements to stars, directors, and the studios that make movies.

Is film school essential?

Not at all. On-the-job training is much more beneficial.

What do you look for when choosing a project?

Simple...something with high energy. Also, finding good characters is very important. A film I recently produced, *Wrestling Ernest Hemingway,* had a lot to do with character. So I would have to say that getting good characters and energy at the same time are important.

JOE WIZAN

What is the most frustrating and then the most gratifying part of producing?

Casting is the most frustrating. It's tough to find the right people you envision. The most gratifying is getting the film done and then when it's a success...that's very gratifying.

Is it crucial for a producer to be involved in casting?

It is critical.

What are the essential skills a producer needs?

Being able to identify good material, having an instinct and having the ability to sell it. The key definition of a producer is to get the movie made. You can't get a movie made without a producer. This is where people skills are very valuable. Getting to know people is as important as getting good material.

Is the producer involved in distribution and marketing?

Totally. I am involved in the beginning of the film until the end. Starting from preproduction to postproduction.

What are your greatest challenges at this stage of your career?

Still getting movies made. That never changes.

Any further advice?

If you have the talent to come to work everyday and get kicked in the balls and come back the next day and do it again, you will succeed. But if you choose not to come to work, nobody cares. You have to do it on your own. You have to have an enormous amount of perseverance.

AFTERWORD

As a recipient of proceeds from the sale of *Making It In Hollywood*, The American Foundation for AIDS Research (AmFAR) gratefully acknowledges the efforts of Gail O'Donnell, Michele Travolta, and participating industry professionals for their roles in the creation of this book and for their dedication to finding enduring solutions to the AIDS pandemic. AmFAR also wishes to acknowledge Dominique Raccah and Sourcebooks, Inc., for their support of this project.

AmFAR is the nation's leading not-for-profit organization dedicated to the support of AIDS research (both basic biomedical research and clinical research), education for AIDS prevention, and sound AIDS-related public policy. Since 1985, AmFAR has provided over $71 million to more than 1,400 research teams. AmFAR mobilizes the goodwill, energy, and generosity of caring Americans to end the AIDS epidemic.

According to estimates by the World Health Organization (WHO), by the year 2000, 40 million people will be infected with HIV, the virus that causes AIDS. AmFAR has been a leading force in the fight against AIDS, and with your support, AmFAR will continue to develop new treatments, bringing us closer to a day without AIDS. Your purchase of this book will help us reach this goal. If you would like more information about AmFAR, or wish to make a direct contribution, please contact us.

Joseph Daniel Green
AmFAR
5900 Wilshire Boulevard, 23rd Floor
Los Angeles, CA 90036
tel: (213) 857-5900

Elizabeth C. Fallon
AmFAR
733 3rd Avenue, 12th Floor
New York, NY 10017
tel: (212) 682-7440

Enjoy These Other Fine Books From Sourcebooks—

Finding Time: Breathing Space For Women Who Do Too Much by Paula Peisner

Learn to successfully manage time and outside demands to find the time to enjoy life more. For every woman too tired, too busy, or just too stressed to think of herself, this bestselling book shows you how to find or make time for yourself.
256 pages, ISBN 0-942061-33-0 (paperback) $7.95

Finding Peace: Letting Go and Liking It by Paula Peisner Coxe

Filled with carefully crafted thoughts, suggestions, and uplifting quotes, *Finding Peace* gives you the opportunity to reassess how you live your life, to contemplate, to forgive, and to accept. From the best-selling author of *Finding Time: Breathing Space For Women Who Do Too Much.*
256 pages, ISBN 1-57071-014-7 (paperback) $7.95

500 Beauty Solutions by Beth Barrick-Hickey

This comprehensive guide provides solutions to the most common hair and nail concerns, plus advice on the hundreds of lotions and potions that line store shelves.
228 pages, ISBN 0-942061-78-0 (paperback) $8.95

Something Old, Something New: What You Didn't Know About Wedding Ceremonies, Celebrations and Customs by Vera Lee

Just what is it that gets you from single to spliced? A ring placed on the finger? The kiss at the altar? The ceremony itself? Learn all this and more as you journey through the many different wedding customs practiced the world around. For all of us who have friends tying or re-tying the knot, this is the perfect wedding gift—something unique for the bride or groom.
228 pages, ISBN 1-57071-002-3 (hardcover) $14.95

Money 101 for the Creatively Inclined: Left-Brain Finance for Right-Brained People by Paula Monroe

Money comes without instructions. This basic money book is specifically written for creative adults who find standard books about personal finance boring and frustrating—page after page of boring print with no visual references. *Money 101 for the Creatively Inclined* is filled with graphs, tables, pictures, anecdotes, and stories to aid those who learn best by using these means for comprehension. The creative person's guide to money management!
350 pages, ISBN 1-57071-017-1 (paperback) $17.95

To order these books or any other of our many publications, please contact your local bookseller or call Sourcebooks at 1-800-727-8866. Get a copy of our catalog by writing or faxing:

Sourcebooks Inc.
P. O. Box 372
Naperville, IL 60566
(708) 961-3900
FAX: (708) 961-2168
Thank you for your interest!

Also Available Are These Fine Business-Related Books From Sourcebooks—

2 Minute Motivation
52 Simple Ways To Manage Your Money
American Banker's Banking Factbook
Attracting The Affluent
Basics Of Finance
Building A Financial Services Marketing Plan
Cash Flow Problem Solver
The Complete Book Of Business Plans
Creating Your Own Future: A Woman's Guide To Retirement Planning
Developing New Financial Products
Electronic Future Of Banking
Financial Services Direct Marketing
Five Star Service Solutions
Future Vision
Getting Paid In Full
How To Get A Loan Or Line Of Credit
How To Market Your Business
How To Sharpen Your Competitive Edge
Insurance Agent's Guide To Telephone Prospecting
The Lifestyle Odyssey
New Age Of Financial Sevices Marketing
Outsmarting The Competition
Practical Marketing Ideas
Protect Your Business
The Small Business Start-Up Guide
The Small Business Survival Guide
Small Claims Court Without A Lawyer
Smart Hiring For Your Business
Soft Sell
Tax Penalties 1991 & Tax Penalties 1992
What To Say When A Customer Complains
Winning
Your First Business Plan

To order these fine books or to receive a catalog, call us at: 1-800-727-8866

Or write to:

Sourcebooks, Inc.
P.O. Box 372
Naperville, IL 60566

1971 $2^u/_{81}$ - $3^u/_{97}$ - $4^u/_{2001}$ - 2 - 3 - 4 - 5 - 6 - 7 - 8 - 9 - 10